NOTHING LEFT TO BURN

Nothing Left to Burn

A MEMOIR | Jay Varner

ALGONQUIN BOOKS OF CHAPEL HILL | 2010

Published by

Algonquin Books of Chapel Hill

Post Office Box 2225

Chapel Hill, North Carolina 27515-2225

a division of

Workman Publishing

225 Varick Street

New York, New York 10014

Printed in the United States of America.

Published simultaneously in Canada

   by Thomas Allen & Son Limited.

Design by Anne Winslow.

Library of Congress Cataloging-in-Publication Data

   Varner, Jay, [date]

      Nothing left to burn : a memoir / Jay Varner. — 1st ed.

         p. cm.

      ISBN 978-1-56512-609-1

      1. Varner, Jay, 1981–   2. McVeytown (Pa.) — Biography.

      3. Children of fire fighters — Pennsylvania — McVeytown —

      Biography.   4. Journalists — Pennsylvania — McVeytown —

      Biography.   5. Fathers and sons — Pennsylvania —

      McVeytown — Biography.   I. Title.

      F159.M24V37 2010

      306.874'2 — dc22   2010002523

10 9 8 7 6 5 4 3 2 1

First Edition

for my father, and for his

We all live in a house on fire, no fire department to call;
no way out, just the upstairs window to look out of while the
fire burns the house down with us trapped, locked in it.
—Tennessee Williams,
The Milk Train Doesn't Stop Here Anymore

Can a man take fire in his bosom,
and his clothes not be burned?
—Proverbs 6:27

NOTHING LEFT TO BURN

Prologue

My grandfather Lucky drove to our trailer every Saturday morning, his silver and maroon Chevrolet pickup loaded with garbage bags piled so high they nearly spilled over the sides. Sometimes the junk was the accumulation of a week's worth of trash from my grandparents' apartment or the old hotel they owned. Or else the truck was full of the unwanted tires, boxes, and newspapers that Lucky offered to dispose of for his friends. I started watching Lucky's Saturday morning ritual when I was five years old.

Each week, I parted the white curtains in our living room window and saw Lucky slowly back his truck up to the edge of a sunken pit, actually the basement of the first house my father had lived in as a child — it sat thirty yards from our trailer and was now filled with brick, cinder blocks, ragged chunks of cement, and junk too rusted to even identify. My mother and I called that spot "the hole."

With a toothpick always plugged in his mouth, Lucky opened the door of the truck and stepped out. He was usually dressed in a white T-shirt, paint-splotched green worker's pants, and scuffed-up leather boots, so cracked they looked as if he had just stomped the entire width of Pennsylvania. Every Saturday he walked across our yard with a hardened and dogged gait, ready to banish anything that stood in his path, and circled the crumbling cinder-block walls of yet another house my father had once lived in with his family. What was left of that building stood five yards north of our trailer and resembled ruins from a war movie.

Lucky stored his caged pigeons inside the damp walls of that second house. I hated those birds. Every time I walked past the building's broken windows, the reveille of coos and fluttering wings spooked me and I feared the birds would somehow burst from the blackness and peck at my face, just like in the Hitchcock movie my mother never let me finish watching on television.

But Lucky loved his pigeons. One winter, he plugged lamps and space heaters into our trailer to warm them, stringing orange extension cords across our yard and inflating our electric bill. He never offered to pay his share.

"We can't afford this," my mother told my dad, waving the bill in front of his face. "What's more important to you, paying to heat your father's pigeons or keeping your family warm?"

My dad must have talked to him because Lucky removed the lamps and heaters without ever saying a word.

But the pigeons weren't alone inside those walls. Rats inhabited the structure too. Sometimes they burrowed under our trailer only to die near the heating vents. When the furnace kicked on, the rats roasted, and the smell sifted through our kitchen and living room. After my mother once complained, Lucky set traps to catch them.

On one Saturday morning, I watched as he emerged from behind the cinder-block wall, holding a bunch of rats by their long, swinging tails. He walked back to his truck and laid the carcasses on the silver bumper.

Then, Lucky lowered the tailgate, stepped up onto the truck, and tossed the black bags of garbage into the hole. Climbing back down, he lifted a five-gallon can of gasoline from the bed and doused the junk with gasoline. When the can was nearly empty, he stepped back from the pile and poured a trail of gas for five or so feet leading from the pit. He grabbed a handful of rats off the truck, and with a flick of his wrist he swung them like lassoes and tossed them into the pit. Next, he lit a match and dropped it to the ground. Flames rose on the path he had poured and then rushed into the garbage, exploding into a wall of fire that flashed up toward the sky. The blaze wheezed a breath of air before releasing a tremendous bang, a sound as loud as my father's hunting rifle, so thunderous that a neighbor some eighty yards away once told my mother that every Saturday morning she could hear the flare-up from inside her house.

Lucky stepped back from the fire, though he still stood so

close that he could probably feel the burn of the heat inside his lungs, and pulled a white hankie from his pocket, patted his bald head, and then swabbed at the back of his hairy neck. He cocked his head like a dog, listening intently, as though the crackle and pop of the flames sounded like a melody to him. He stood with his arms crossed and stared at his fire, never moving until the last flame died out.

Part One

One

Halfway through August, a heat wave sinks into central Pennsylvania, and it feels like the countryside is sealed inside a clammy Mason jar. Sweat trickles down my back as I smoke a cigarette to calm my nerves. I have been hired as a reporter for my hometown newspaper. It's my first night. I lean against the brown bricks outside the single-story building that houses the *Sentinel* and wish for a breeze or thunderstorm—anything that might funnel relief into the soupy air—but I know that none will come. The sky is mottled with haze. I toss my cigarette down into a metal coffee can, a makeshift ashtray half full of spent butts, and open the back door.

Just two days earlier I had somehow convinced Elizabeth, the newspaper's editor, that I have the "nose for journalism" the advertisement for a reporter's position demanded. I know how to write a story, I told her, leaving out the fact that I had taken only one journalism class in college. I told her there are the sacred five *Ws* — who, what, where, when, why — but beyond that, there are human stories. These are real people with real lives and I would be indebted to tell the truth. When I stood to leave, Elizabeth shook my hand and apologized about forgetting my scheduled interview; I wore a suit and tie while she stood in purple sweatpants and a T-shirt silk-screened with butterflies.

My first afternoon at the *Sentinel,* Elizabeth leads me through the newspaper's small office. The low ceilings hold buzzing fluorescent lights — there seem to be no shadows cast onto the worn, brown carpet. The only natural light that seeps into the building comes from the glass facade at the front of the building. However, none of that light makes it to the newsroom because it is eclipsed by the tall, carpeted walls of cubicles that make up the advertising department.

Elizabeth introduces me to my fellow reporters, then finally shows me to my cubicle. The walls are waist high and it feels as spacious as a shoe box. Sitting on the desk is a computer that looks to be fifteen years old, perhaps a remnant from the Reagan administration. Next to the computer sits a police and fire scanner that beeps every few minutes, just like the red Motorola pager my father used to clip on his leather belt. A streak of tones, vacillating in pitch and frequency, whine from the tiny black scanner. Dread singes my nerves — I know that sound too well already.

"Why the scanner?" I ask.

"Figured we'll start you out on police and fire," Elizabeth

says. She narrows her eyes, as if examining me. "That'll be okay, right?"

"Sure," I say. "Yeah, that's no problem."

As I stare at that scanner, I think of my father who had been McVeytown's volunteer fire chief. Each time I pass the McVeytown Volunteer Fire Company and see a few of the guys standing outside, I don't swell with the pride that most people in small towns feel for their volunteer firemen—I feel the same way about them as I feel about my father. Those men abandon their families. The firehouse was my dad's excuse to miss dinner, skip out on my elementary school's open houses, and break plans to play baseball or take me fishing. His commitment to his job as fire chief exceeded expectations—it seemed a guttural obsession, perhaps an addiction.

My dad left home for fires, car accidents, flooded basements, company meetings, seminars, training exercises, and conventions. Even when he worked himself raw cutting glass at his factory job and complained of sore joints and bloody knuckles and stomach problems, when he was called he bolted to his feet and went out to save the day, like one of the superheroes I watched on afternoon cartoons.

He jumped from his chair at dinner, lunged out of bed in the night. He raced past cars on the highway in his pickup truck—the red strobe light on the roof flashing, the speedometer climbing, sometimes my mother and I sitting beside him and grasping the vinyl seat. One such day, he pulled into the firehouse parking lot, slamming on the brake and jerking the truck to a sudden stop. He popped the door, jumped down, and ran toward the station house.

"Just drive it home," he yelled to my mother before he dashed into the engine room.

It was scary, amd sometimes frustrating, but there was something exciting about it as well. It was as if he kept the entire town safe, as if somehow none of us could survive without him.

My complicated history with fire seems unknown to my newsroom co-workers, many of whom are in their early thirties and probably never even heard of Denton Varner, my father. But lots of other people in Mifflin County still love him and consider him a hero. Fewer people remember, or perhaps conveniently forget, that my grandfather Lucky loved to ignite fires. I don't say a word to Elizabeth about my family's past, afraid that if I decline the police and fire beat, I will be fired from a job that I desperately need. Most of my friends in the class of 2003 began working jobs when we graduated three months earlier — places like insurance companies, corporate front offices, and national magazines. None of them still live in their hometown and write for their local daily newspapers.

Later that first night, I learn how to write obituaries.

Ken, the newsroom clerk, sits next to me as I type my first batch of obits. He tells me the formula on how to write up the dead. The most important things come first: name, age, address, and time and place of death. Then a new paragraph for the background: date of birth, place of birth, parents, and spouse. The next paragraph lists the survivors. There is an order to this laundry list of family members as well: The most important (usually the children) come first. Aunts, uncles, or cousins come last. The rest fall somewhere in between. There are exact rules, wordings, and euphemisms that must be followed.

Ken scratches his goatee while I type. He seems to genuinely enjoy the order of death. Faxes from the funeral homes provide the specifics of the deceased. All I have to do is arrange the information.

"We used to include the words *public viewing,*" Ken says. "But now it's *friends may call* instead. Someone who was doing these forgot a letter once and wrote *pubic* instead of *public.* The family didn't like that."

"This is bitch work, isn't it?" I ask. "The lowest job for a reporter?"

"Look at it this way," he says, and taps a finger on the desk. "You're guaranteed to have your stuff read. People want to know who died. They read these obituaries every day."

When I finish for the night, I walk through the newsroom, past the tiny lunch room and the cubicles of the circulation department, and slip out the back door for a cigarette. The night looks still and haunted. A fat moon, two days past its prime, spills a blue tint over the wooded knob of a nearby hill and washes down onto the parking lot. Lightning bugs glow to life, then fade, like the flashing beacons of the radio relay towers stuck on distant ridges. In a few weeks the fireflies will disappear from the night along with the heat. It feels as if everything will go out with the summer but me.

One of the guys from the press room opens the door and steps outside for a breath of air. His blue uniform clings to the heft of his frame. Ink stains his fingers and forearms.

"We got a name for you already," he says. "Clark Kent."

"Well, I am wearing red underwear, but I'd need a cape."

"No, it's the glasses," he says, pointing to my trendy, black-rimmed frames. "What beat do they have you working?"

"Police and fire. And writing obits."

"I've seen so many people go through that desk," he says. "I've just stopped learning their names. I've been here thirty years and let me tell you something—you'll be gone in a year."

"You think so?"

"I know so," he says. "You burn out on that beat."

I had already burned out on Mifflin County—I never even wanted to return here.

Many people in my family had not gone to college and the ones who did had attended state universities, not liberal arts schools as I had done. Though tuition had been expensive, I relied on financial aid, student loans, and grants. Most of my family worked practical jobs—they dug ditches along the railroad, reviewed loans at banks, or taught middle school. I was raised believing that college was the ultimate privilege, something sacred that should never be wasted. With that attitude, my family couldn't understand what I would possibly pursue with a degree in creative writing. None of them had a penchant for the arts—they enjoyed things like hunting deer and turkey, fishing for trout and rock bass, or watching baseball and football. To me, moving back home was my admission of defeat, a declaration that their concerns had been justified and that my four years at college had been wasted. Here comes the prodigal son, I imagined them saying, crawling back home with his tail between his legs.

And so, on graduation day, I swallowed my pride and packed up my dorm room, loaded everything into the car, and moved back home with my mother. There was no party and no cake, just the two of us quietly watching television together that Sunday night. The place still looked exactly as I had remembered it—there was not much room, even for two people. We couldn't even walk past each other in the hallway by turning sideways—someone had to step into the bathroom or bedrooms until the other passed. And no matter where I went—my bedroom, the corner office I had set up in the basement to write, or the front porch—I could hear every move she made. The floors squeaked and moaned as if the house were alive. I yearned for the privacy of my dorm room, which had actually been quieter.

But my mother seemed happy to have me home. We took walks together in the evenings. Once a week we mowed the lawn—she drove the riding mower, while I circled trees with the push mower. She told me things that needed to be fixed—the clothesline, a bench on the porch, the door to the shed—and I made sure they were repaired to her liking. On Sunday nights we ordered a pizza from Jimmy's Pizza, McVeytown's only attempt at anything resembling an Italian restaurant, and then watched baseball together.

"You know," she said one night, "you're going to have to get a job soon."

"I know."

"What were you thinking of doing?"

"Something will work out," I said.

"When are you thinking of looking for a job?" she asked.

"I looked," I said. "There's not much open right now."

"Wal-Mart's hiring again." She raised her eyebrows and waited for my response.

During college, I worked three summers at Wal-Mart, barely

making above the minimum wage. It was bad enough then, but now that I had a degree, there was no way I would work there again.

That summer dragged on, but then I opened the newspaper and saw an advertisement for a reporting position with the *Sentinel*. It didn't seem like such a bad job. Maybe it would make living in Mifflin County a bearable experience.

The area, located almost directly between Philadelphia and Pittsburgh, once thrived on agriculture and industry but now suffered in irrelevance. I had grown up in McVeytown, a blink-and-you-miss-it town that had only one store at which to buy groceries, one gas station, and two restaurants. Alfalfa and corn-fields surrounded everything; they rolled out like long tracts of green and brown carpet before meeting the undulating ridges on the horizon, part of the Appalachian Mountains' long stretch through central Pennsylvania. At dusk, sunset fired the dairy farms in a golden hue and burnished the surface of the Juniata River. The silence of night was broken by the distant wail of a freight train as it beat and clanked along the railroad tracks, or by the machine-gunning Jake Brakes on the semis rolling on Route 522 through McVeytown.

Lewistown, the largest town in Mifflin County and home to the *Sentinel* office, was fifteen miles east of McVeytown and had seemed like a city when I was a kid, when I thought that I wanted to live here for the rest of my life. This was when in-dustrial plants still clustered along the snaking Juniata River, a waterway that once transported tons of goods each day as part of the Pennsylvania Canal, back before railroad lines veined over fields and roads. Back then, factories that produced airplane parts, stereos, televisions, automobile seats, cabinets, and candy surrounded the town. Family-owned storefronts surrounded the town square.

But like so many small towns across the country, the stranglehold of Wal-Mart spread like cancer. The stores closest to "Wally World" shut down first, then the ones on the square, and finally people had two choices: shop at Wal-Mart or don't shop at all. Around this same time, the first of the factories began to close.

It wasn't just the jobs that left—people did too. Since the 1960s, Lewistown's population had decreased by 29 percent. Around twelve thousand resided in the borough in 1973. By the time I returned to Mifflin County after college, only eight thousand were left within the city limits. And though there were fewer people competing for employment openings, even dead-end jobs became increasingly difficult to find. The options for high school graduates ebbed. Grandfathers, fathers, and sons who had defined themselves by their lineage at the same manufacturing plants searched for something different to do. Their jobs went away but the old factories were left standing, mausoleums of the town's industrial past. The buildings' windows were boarded up; the insides stripped, boxed, and shipped overseas. Parking lots the size of football fields sat empty.

For the past several years, my dream has been to escape all of this, yet I accepted a job at the *Sentinel* because Elizabeth offered to hire me, because I was too scared to turn it down, because I don't know what else to do with my life. When I graduated college, I believed that I had overcome the negative pull of my past and that my family's history of fascination with fire no longer haunted me. But now I think I am wrong about that. I know that working the police and fire beat will unearth memories I buried long ago, and that I will ultimately have to face the unsettling memory of my father.

After work that first night, I drive on the narrow back roads between Lewistown and McVeytown, headed home where I know my mother will still be awake. I pull into our driveway and watch as a half-dozen cats scatter in my headlights. My mom has opened all the windows to our home, a double-wide trailer, which feels like the inside of a kiln at the height of summer. Most of my college friends know only that I live in a small house—I was usually too embarrassed to admit the truth and tip off people about my social class. Even a girlfriend in college believed it for two years before she finally visited for a week one summer.

"How'd it go?" my mother asks. She stands at the kitchen sink and dries her hands on a dish towel. Her face looks flushed and hot.

"Fine," I say. "They want me to work the police and fire beat."

"That's not so bad, is it?" She smiles and I notice how few wrinkles she has. She thinks forty-six is old, though I tell her that most of my friends have parents who are already sixty.

I sit at the dining room table and shake my head. "I have to go out on calls. I have to go to the fires and talk with victims. Would you want to do that?"

She doesn't say anything for a while. She finishes her work at the sink and then sits on the love seat in the dining room. Her fingers pick at frays of itchy upholstering.

"It won't be that bad, will it?" she asks.

"It's a job," I say.

"Around here, you're lucky to get one of those," she says. "Going out on fire calls. Well, I'm sure you dad would find that interesting."

Two

On some evenings, I rode into McVeytown with my father, usually to buy milk or bread. My dad's heavy steel-toed boots pounded up the rickety wooden steps outside Kline's Market. He pulled open the heavy glass door and I followed him inside. These trips should have taken ten minutes, but for my dad they lasted an hour. Usually, we saw some of his friends: firemen, police officers, reporters, or co-workers. They always smiled when they saw him. They were tall, thick men, not unlike my dad, who wore hats and mustaches like him. They even dressed the same: scuffed steel-toed boots, grease-stained and faded blue jeans, and solid-color T-shirts. All of them wanted to talk with my father.

One night, my father's best friend, Art Kenmore, was in the store. The two worked together at a factory called Overhead

Door, and both volunteered with the fire company. Art stood in line at the meat counter at the back of the store and stared at cuts of chipped ham, Lebanon bologna, and farmer's cheese, as if studying them for a test.

My father looked down at me and pressed a finger against his lips. He slowly walked up behind Art and stuck a finger into Art's shoulder blade.

"Give me your wallet," my dad said softly.

Art, his eyes wide and scared, snapped his head around. When he saw my father, he smiled, exposing the gap between his two front teeth. He shook his head.

"You almost scared me half to death," Art said.

"What happens if you scare someone half to death twice?" my father asked. "Ever think about that?"

Art rolled his eyes and pointed at the meat counter. "I'm trying to decide what I want for lunch tomorrow. Sally forgot to buy meat when she went grocery shopping."

"Teena wanted me to come down for some milk," my dad said. He yanked at the bill of his hat and wiggled it back and forth on his head.

Art rested his hands on his knees and leaned forward, peering down at me. "How's first grade?"

"It's still there," I said, remembering one of my father's oft-recited answers.

Art slapped his thigh and stood straight. "Smart aleck. Wonder where he gets that?"

"Hey, what do you call cows with a sense of humor?" my father asked. "Laughing stock."

Art and I both laughed. My dad loved jokes. Every night, he

told my mother and me jokes that he had heard during lunch at work. And each time he saw one of his friends, they traded jokes for a few minutes. Sometimes it seemed like a kind of secret language to me because I didn't understand them, even though I still laughed. But when I did get his jokes, I felt part of the separate world he shared with his friends.

"You know what would happen if you lined up all the cars in the world end to end?" Art asked. "Someone would be stupid enough to try to pass them."

My dad softly laughed and thought for a moment. "Hey, you hear about the Energizer Bunny?"

"Yeah, he was arrested for battery."

My dad raised his eyebrows and cocked his head back. "Did I tell you that already?"

"At work the other day," Art said. "Your mind must be slipping in old age."

"Hey now," my dad said. He pointed a finger at Art. "Growing old is mandatory. Growing up isn't."

At the checkout counter, my dad talked with the cashier for a few minutes about the new house she and her husband were building. Like the jokes that made little sense to me, I didn't understand talk of framing walls, underlayment, and foam channel insulation. But I nodded as my father talked, as if I agreed with all that he said.

"Remember to remind him to bury that drainage pipe away from any disturbed earth. Now that might be five or six feet from the foundation." He said it with such force and passion that anyone who disagreed would have seemed ignorant.

"And that's better?" the cashier asked. She furrowed her brow as if she was trying to understand the terms as well.

"Oh, you better believe it," my dad said. "If you install that pipe on uncompacted ground, it'll get a negative pitch and then the runoff water will flow the wrong way. It might be a little harder for him to lay the pipe in fresh ground, but it'll give both of you piece of mind knowing that it's going to work."

The cashier stared at my father a moment and then smiled. "How do you know all this, Denton?"

He shrugged. "I just know a little something about everything. But I'll tell you this: if he doesn't do the pipe that way, I can guarantee you the fire company will be out there next time it rains and we'll have to pump that basement. You tell him to call me if he has any questions."

"I'll let him know, Denton. Thanks."

In the parking lot, he lifted me into the passenger side of his truck and made sure I buckled my seat belt before he started the engine. A pickup passed on the street. The driver tooted the horn and waved at my father.

"Who was that?" I asked.

"I don't even know," my dad said. "Guess they like me, though, huh?"

My dad seemed like the most famous man in town. People recognized his beat-up Ford F-150 and the knobby red strobe light that clung to the roof. Rusted running boards hung along the sides of the truck. A toolbox, painted a muddy brown primer that matched the body of the truck, spanned the bed at the end closest to the cab and held his mismatched screwdrivers, battered hammers, a nicked crowbar, spare gloves, a first-aid kit, flares, and an ax. Most importantly, the box stored his fire gear — a helmet and his canvaslike jacket so heavy that it nearly pulled me to the ground when I tried it on.

"That's what I wear every time I go to a fire," he said as he buckled the rings of the coat around me. It felt like he was sealing me inside. "These are called D rings. If you don't hook these in a fire, the heat is so intense, it'll burn your skin right off."

"Could that happen to you?" I asked.

He smiled. "Me? No, I'm a pro. I'm the chief. Been wearing turn-out gear for years now. And pretty soon you'll be strong enough to wear it too."

In a way, I understood what he meant. When I was strong enough to wear that gear, then I would be a man like my father, and then maybe all of the people in town would want to talk to me just like they wanted to talk to him. I would enter that other world my father lived in, that place where he spent so much of his time away from home.

For all the talents that my father had — telling jokes, giving advice on everything from repairing engines to building a house, and fighting fires — he was best at leaving. By kindergarten, I could recite his schedule as well as the alphabet: ambulance meetings on Monday nights, work detail Tuesday nights, company meetings on Wednesdays, and in between all of that, emergency management meetings throughout the county. His pager sounded at all hours, summoning him from work, dinner, or sleep.

During the days, my dad cut glass at Overhead Door. When he stopped at the firehouse every afternoon on his way home from work, he parked along the highway so everyone in town could see that he was on call. The building that housed the McVeytown Volunteer Fire Company had two garage doors and a sheet metal exterior that was painted an off-green. The building looked flimsy, nothing like the massive stone firehouses that I had seen on television. The small banquet hall—where my parents had their wedding reception—flanked one side of the building. In the back of the building was a large gravel-covered parking lot.

When my father parked in front of the firehouse, he said that it was a reminder of his dedication. His priorities had always been clear: the fire department came first; everything else was second. This was how most people of McVeytown thought of him; Denton Varner was a husband and father, a loyal friend, a good driver, and a fan of trivia, but most of all he was their fire chief.

Sometimes my dad drove my mother and me to McDonald's where he ordered me a Happy Meal. McDonald's is the only place other than home I remember us ever eating at. When a Pizza Hut opened in Lewistown, some of my friends at school talked about going there with their parents. The next time we went to McDonald's, I decided to suggest something different.

"Dad, can we go to Pizza Hut instead?" I asked. "My friends said it's really cool."

"Mmm, it'd probably take too long," he said.

"Too long for what?"

"To get our food," he said. "If there's a call, I have to be able to jump up and just go. Pizza Hut's one of those places where you have to pay at the end of your meal."

"Oh. Okay." If my father needed to leave at a moment's notice, then he must be important. I thought of Batman and how Commissioner Gordon flashed the bat signal in the sky—my father's pager was his signal.

When my father was at home, he spent much of his time outdoors working or mowing the lawn. The orange and red Case riding lawn mower was too small for my father—his knees stuck out, and he looked like a man riding a child's toy. He wore blue jeans, a pocketed T-shirt, and one of his trucker's hats with the bulldog of the Mack truck logo on the front. Large ear protectors clung to his head as though he were about to go skeet shooting. "Always shield your ears," he once told me after I asked why he wore the clunky things. My mother then told me the real reason: an earpiece was plugged into his pager to feed him the emergency codes if a call came.

One evening, I watched my father mow the lawn from my perch atop the metal slide he had assembled for me. The onion-sweet smell of freshly cut grass hung thick in the humid air. As he steered the mower, he smiled under his mustache and waved. But then the smile faded. He shut the mower off, held his hands to his ear protectors, and I knew that he was listening to a dispatcher report a fire. He jumped up, threw the ear protectors onto the mower seat, and ran across the yard.

I plunged down the slide. When my feet hit the ground, I ran toward his pickup but he had already climbed inside.

"Can I go with you?" I asked.

He turned on the engine and gunned the gas.

"Dad, please, can I go? Please."

He didn't even look down at me. "No," he said, hard and loud.

The truck bounced and shook as my father drove over our cracked macadam driveway and then sped out of sight.

Lots of times when he left like that I waited atop that slide and watched for his headlights to surface on the slight hill above our house. My skin got clammy in the soupy and still air. Far off in the distance a freight train beat over the tracks and echoed against the ridges. I waited there for him until long after lightning bugs first pinholed the darkness of night.

"Jay," my mother called from the porch. "It's time for bed."

I sank down the slide and walked across the yard. I changed into my pajamas and climbed into bed. My mother tucked the sheets under my arms.

"Why does Dad always have to leave?"

"What?" She sat on the edge of the bed.

"Why can't he just stay home with us?"

My mother stared at the floor, silent for a moment. "He's the chief," she said.

"Why does he have to be the fire chief?"

"Because he likes to help people," she said. She looked at the floor and smiled. "And people like him. The fire company elected him."

"Couldn't they have elected someone else?" I asked. "Don't you miss him?"

"Sure I do," she said. "I wish that he was here more too. But he's not. He's got his job to do at the firehouse. And you know your father. He'll want to make sure it gets done right."

Hot tears streamed down my cheeks. She patted my head.

"He'll be back soon," she said. And then, as if to convince herself, she said it again: "He'll be back soon. You go to sleep."

She stood, kissed my head, and closed the door behind her. But I lay awake every night he wasn't home, sometimes until the bruised light of dawn washed over the room. I lay there and waited for the roar of his truck to pull into the driveway and his boots to stomp up the wooden porch steps.

I had seen him return home in the daylight and knew what to expect: the collars of his shirts were grimy with salt from his sweat. Soot smeared his face and hands. The stale smell of smoke clung to his clothes. During those long night waits, I sometimes imagined that he would open my bedroom door, sit on the bed next to me, turn on my dresser lamp, and talk to me.

But this never happened—not this night or the hundreds of others like it. Instead, he showered and then climbed in bed next to my mother to sleep before waking at 6:00 a.m. to head to work at Overhead Door. And I lay there in the dark.

My dad first volunteered for the junior fireman program when he was in high school. His classmates mentioned it in his senior yearbook—some thanked him for his work; others warned him not to get too involved. Some thirty years after he graduated, I read through some letters and cards classmates had sent my father. A friend named Rick wrote my dad a postcard in 1972. Rick had traveled to Disney World, and he told my father he had looked for the Disney World fire company—he wanted a picture to send to my dad. Rick also signed the back of his senior photo for my father, writing, "Don't forget all the good times we had at the fire hall and other places (hint, hint). Keep the town from burning down." Another friend named Jan wrote a similar note on his class picture: "Have fun in the future, but you shouldn't get so carried away with fires (how many days has it been since a fire?)."

His might have been the most recognizable face in town, even back then. When he earned his Eagle Scout badge in the Boy Scouts, the *Sentinel* printed a snapshot from the ceremony — appearing in the *Sentinel* was the true testament of fame in any of the surrounding small towns. My dad had yet to grow his mustache in that grainy sepia photo. He wore wire-rimmed, round-lensed eyeglasses and had his hair fashioned in a bowl cut. Something about that look always reminded me of a folk singer — maybe because he had played guitar in a band with his older brothers, Curt and Russ, and a few of their friends, performing at churches and parties around town.

By the time my dad graduated high school, his brothers had already moved away — Curt to Ohio, Russ to Delaware. My father, however, was not tempted to leave. He immersed himself deeper in the life of a fireman. He dispatched emergency calls, spending long hours alone at the station house and waiting for the phone to ring. He enrolled in classes and earned his emergency medical technician certification.

In 1979, my dad moved back to the same acre or so of land outside McVeytown where he had grown up. He had married my mother by then and they wanted to start a family. Though my father had bought the single-wide trailer he lived in with my mother and me, the land that it sat upon was still owned by

Lucky, who had refused to lend my father money to buy property, and instead let my father use the former plot of his childhood home. Unable to afford anything else, my father accepted the offer but made a deal with himself: one day, he would build a proper house for his family, not some "rinky-dink trailer," and he would do it on his own piece of land.

Three piles of rubble scarred that ground we lived upon. If I stepped onto the front porch of the trailer, I saw the hole, that sunken pit where my grandfather burned his trash on Saturday mornings. When I stepped onto the trailer's back porch and looked east, I saw the foundation of Lucky's old workshop some twenty yards away—the building was gone now, and a few saplings knifed through the broken concrete floor. Five yards north of our trailer, the remnants of the other house still stood; the cold cinder-block walls that housed Lucky's pigeons. These three foundations formed the end points of a triangle—our trailer sat in the center.

But the surrounding natural beauty almost compensated for the debris. Blue ridges of the mountains humped on the horizon and overlooked farm fields whose crops were divided as neatly as patches on a quilt—in the snowy winter, those ridges looked as though they were topped with whipped cream. Oak and English walnut trees shaded our lawn in the summertime. A pear, a cherry, and four apple trees flanked our neighbor's hog pasture along the far end of the yard. These provided spots for the tree house I had begged my father to build.

"That'd be pretty neat, huh?" he said. "One of these days, I'll build one for you."

Three

My dad and I sat inside the stuffy cab of a restored 1954
Ford Oren pumper fire truck—the chrome polished, the cherry
red chassis waxed. We parked outside McVeytown on a narrow
road. Sitting on a slight rise, we looked down on the spectacle
before us: the Lewistown Area High School marching band
stood at the front of the half-mile-long parade procession, followed by antique cars, their bodies glinting under the sun, and
John Deere tractors hitched to floats, one of which carried the
Mifflin County Dairy Princess. The vehicles' engines churned,
clotting the afternoon with exhaust and noise.

In only its first year, Country Memories Day already seemed a
success in McVeytown. Food vendors arrived at the fairgrounds
at dawn and assembled stands to sell hot sausage sandwiches

and funnel cakes. Mennonites set up tables around the town square and displayed homemade cookies, bread, and whoopee pies, a Pennsylvania Dutch specialty—two chocolate cakes with a creamy frosting between them. Townspeople opened their garage doors, ready to sell quilts, antiques, wicker baskets, and knickknacks. It went on like this for hours, capped in the afternoon by the pageantry of a parade through town.

"What time does the parade start?" I asked.

"Three," my father said. He flicked his wrist and glanced at his Timex Ironman watch. "We still have a few minutes yet."

He was tall and slender, dressed in a white, starched short-sleeved shirt with ironed creases. A black tie, perfectly knotted and pinched in the middle by a silver clip, hung from his neck. He wore black pants held up by a slim dress belt that matched his shoes, both a radiant midnight black, polished to a sheen that looked wet to the touch. Had it not been for the silver badge pinned over his right breast, my father might have been mistaken for one of those dapper Jehovah's Witnesses who sometimes knocked on our door. He thought he looked spiffy, a term he always used to describe his dress uniform. And Country Memories Day was the perfect chance to show off in front of the entire town.

In the distance, the blue and white uniforms of the marching band lurched forward—I heard their faint horns and drums. The cars and tractors followed, huffing diesel fumes into the hot air. Finally, my father stomped on the clutch and shifted the truck into first gear.

"Ready to get this show on the road, kiddo?" he asked. He pressed the gas and we jerked forward.

We came dead last in the parade procession, the best part to a six-year-old. Each year, I had watched on television as Santa Claus waved to the crowds from the final float in the Macy's Thanksgiving Day parade. Since my father and I came at the end, I thought that we were the most important part of this parade.

We rolled past the playground, where the Babe Ruth and Little League teams played, and turned left onto Vine Street. Spectators watched the parade go by—some sat on lawn chairs, others stood shoulder to shoulder with their neighbors. Nearly all of them waved at my father or shouted his name. He waved back and smiled like a candidate running for office.

"Hey Denton, who's that in there with you?" someone asked.

"Our new recruit," my father yelled out the window. "A little young, but he'll grow into it."

As we rolled through town, I craned my neck and peered over the dash. From the cab of the truck the world appeared to be far below us. We passed the old Rothrock High School, closed eleven years earlier, just after my father graduated. Wild webs of ivy now suffocated the dark brick walls. It looked haunted, like the kind of place forever stuck in the past. I wondered what my father had been like when he went there.

"Like riding in here?" my father asked.

"Yeah. It's so big."

"Well, if you think this is big you should ride in the tanker or the engine sometime," he said. "Maybe next year we'll do that. But to drive a rig like this someday, you'll have to know how to shift."

"Shift?" I asked.

"Some trucks need to be put into different gears in order to go faster or slower. You just put your foot on this pedal down here called a clutch and move this stick in the floor."

"Dad, my feet can't even reach the floor."

"I know, I know, but I'll teach you this someday when you learn how to drive. Here." He gently grabbed my left hand and rested it on the knob at the end of the stick. "This is called the gear shift."

His large palm cupped the back of my hand.

"Just get a grip on it, step on the clutch and move it like this."

His long leg stamped on the clutch, and when he pushed the stick forward, our hands moved together as if we were one.

As the parade rolled slowly on, we passed the Lutheran and Methodist churches and then the town library. The crowds continued to wave, and at my father's encouragement, I did too. My father, his right hand on the gear shift, his other on the wheel, looked at me and nodded as if I were doing a good job. Ahead of us, people clustered around the town square. The flag flew high against the crisp blue sky. It seemed that we were moving in slow motion until something suddenly banged against the passenger side door. I flinched, jerking away from the open window.

My grandfather Lucky climbed onto the running board of the moving truck and poked his head into the cab. His face always set off a surge of fear in my chest. Behind Lucky's Buddy Holly glasses were beady birdlike eyes that rarely blinked, and he stared at me in the same way a mannequin stares through a storefront window, with a still and fixed expression. For Lucky, that expression was a smirk, as if he had just told off the smartest man in town.

"Got a little fireman in here with you?" He asked the question as if provoked, in sharp whiplike cracks. "What's the matter with you, boy?"

He reached into the cab and grabbed my arm with his calloused hand. "You're never going to be strong enough to be a fireman with those muscles." His lips curled in a sneer and sweat glistened on his bald head.

I squirmed out of his reach and slid across the seat next to my father. Lucky stared for a moment and then winked at me.

"Be nice if the boy took after you, wouldn't it, Dent?"

"Oh, Jay's just along for the ride, Dad. At least for today."

"I'll bet he wants to be a fireman just like his old man." Lucky stared at me and lurched further inside the cab, resting his elbows on the window frame and hunching his shoulders. "Think you want to be a fireman?"

I stared ahead, hoping that if I didn't answer he'd leave me alone.

He poked my shoulder as though checking to see if I was still alive. "You need to stop acting so shy. Start talking once in a while."

Lucky raised a hand, pretending to be ready to give me a backhand slap across the mouth. I flinched and looked up at my father—he waved at the crowd, ignoring my grandfather.

Then Lucky leaned back out the window and jumped down off the truck. I slid back to my original position and peeked over the window frame.

Lucky, his long legs swiveling, stepped over the wooden sawhorses meant for crowd control. He then stood next to my grandmother Helen, who was wearing one of her too-tight dresses and looked upon the parade with an open mouth. She clasped her purse and smiled at Lucky. Many people still regarded Lucky as one of the best carpenters in Mifflin County even though he was in his midsixties. He fingered a toothpick from the front pocket of his shirt, stuck it in his mouth, and stared hard at the truck.

Sometimes when my dad was at the firehouse, my mother told me stories about my grandparents—she never attempted to hide her dislike for her in-laws. When Lucky and Helen visited, my mother sat on a recliner in the living room, her arms folded across her chest, her jaw clenched, speaking only if Helen or Lucky asked her a question.

During my birth, my mother and I had both contracted staph infections at the hospital and nearly died. We spent weeks recuperating at the house of my mother's parents, under doctor's orders to have few visitors. Lucky finally saw me, his first grandchild, over two months later. My mother told me he stared at me with his usual smirk.

"Look at his little hands," he said. "Look like monkey's paws."

Helen had come along with Lucky—she seemed to never go anywhere without him. She gave my mother baby clothes. When my mother unfolded the sweaters and coveralls, she saw that they were stained.

"I saw them at a yard sale along the road on the way here," Helen said.

"Figured he'd just stain them again anyway," Lucky said. "What's the sense of buying something new only to have them ruined?"

My mother always told that story in disbelief. "You were their first grandchild," she said. "And they couldn't even buy you new clothes."

To me, these seemed slight offenses compared to the terror I felt whenever I was near Lucky. He always called me "boy" and I always thought of him as Lucky, never as Grandpa. When he came to visit, Lucky usually asked me about school, but before I could answer, he told a story of his own boyhood in an attempt to one-up me. "The teachers sometimes sent me home halfway through the school day because I was so smart," he told me. "They figured that I'd learned all that they could teach and that I slowed the other kids down."

I never believed any of his stories. He said that one time, after a hard rain, he was driving home but couldn't see the road for a mile and a half because toads completely blanketed the pavement — "should've heard them pop under the tires." He said that he often dived from the river bridge in Lewistown to cool down on sticky summer days. Each time I went to Lewistown with my parents, I looked at the depth meter painted on the side of one of the bridge's trestles. If his story was true, Lucky would have endured a seventy-foot freefall into the Juniata River, usually only two or three feet deep at the peak of summer.

But those were just stories. Harmless. Nothing compared to the fires I watched him light on Saturday mornings. I muffled my ears with my hands, anticipating the loud pop from the explosion, a sound so thunderous it seemed to reverberate through my stomach. The stink of the smoke seeped through the trailer, a scent that hung stagnant inside the tiny space for hours afterward—it was how my father smelled after he returned from fighting a fire. And Lucky's burns weren't just restricted to Saturdays—at any moment, he could turn into our driveway, his left arm hanging out the open window, the bed of the truck filled with whatever he had found that would ignite. "Cheaper to burn than pay for trash collection," he said once.

Sometimes my mother stood next to me and we both watched his custom of culling the dead rats and then laying them on his bumper.

"After you were born, I was so afraid of that man," my mother told me one Saturday morning. "I was terrified that he'd come here and burn you or this trailer. One time he asked for a glass of water when he came to check on his pigeons. I gave it to him but didn't let him inside because your dad wasn't home. He handed me the glass and said, 'Glad you let me have this. I'm not so bad, huh?' But before he left, he leaned toward me and said, 'But how do you know? I could be contemplating murdering you right now.'"

Her stories made me fear him even more. Something dark seemed buried inside him, a hatred or anger that could blow with little prodding. Once, when I was very young, Lucky slapped our Dalmatian, Patches, on the head after she put her feet on his lap—the dog whimpered to the floor and Lucky nodded, as if he had taught her a lesson. I realized then that he would do the same to me, or to my mother. There would be no difference.

After the flames had burned out on those Saturday mornings, he stepped into his truck and drove away. And those times when he hadn't thrown them into the fire, the dead rats he had placed on his bumper littered the road.

Four

Just after New Year's Day 1988, my dad began talking about living somewhere else. It started during a blustery night when my parents and I watched television together. I sat sandwiched between them on a secondhand couch that Helen and Lucky had given us. My Christmas break had ended—the second half of my first grade year started the next day. My dad slouched next to me, arms crossed, eyes focused on the small, fuzzy television screen. He wore a flannel shirt, faded Levi's, and one of those mesh hats that he seemed to take off only when he showered or went to bed. My mother, also in flannel, was nodding off to sleep. We had learned to dress in layers or else spend the winter shivering. Though I wore long johns under my corduroys and sweatshirt, I felt my legs and arms goose-pimple from the ever-present draft. The wind hissed through cracks in the window frames. Branches on the oak trees next to our trailer raked against one another and creaked like rusty hinges. A gust roared outside and something crashed onto the trailer's metal roof.

My mother snapped awake. "Denton, what was that?" she asked. Her voice quivered, matching her shallow breaths. "What in the world was it?"

My dad hadn't even flinched and continued to stare at the television. He rolled his eyes. "I'll check once this is over."

"Go see what it was," she said.

He huffed and said, "Fine." He stood, marched down the dark hallway to their bedroom, put on his down coat, and then grabbed one of his Maglite flashlights on the nightstand.

After he opened the back door, he paused and pointed a finger at the television. "Make sure you watch that," he said. "I want to know what happens." He stepped outside and slammed the door shut.

In the winter, weekly storms dumped clean snow onto the already frosted landscape, white-blanketing everything outside. Afternoon squalls added fresh dustings that rolled with the blowing wind. Storm gusts smacked against our trailer. We felt the whole thing sway like a boat even though my father had placed an old out-of-tune upright piano in the living room as ballast. Frigid air leaked through the single-paned windows, and the oil furnace hummed in vain to overtake the cold. Our kitchen sat in the middle of the trailer, cramped with the round dinner table. No wall or partition separated it from the living room. A hallway, too narrow for my parents to stand side by side, led to my bedroom, the bathroom, and then my parents' room. My father called the trailer a "tin can" and said that sooner or later the wind would blow the place onto its side.

When I heard that crash on the roof, I wondered if the wind was finally going to blow the trailer over like my father had warned. I barely breathed for fear that any movement would throw the entire place off balance. "Are we going to be okay?" I whispered.

My mother pulled me close and hugged me. "Don't worry. Your dad will take care of it."

After a few minutes, he stepped back inside. His reddened cheeks looked minutes away from frostbite or windburn. "Just a branch," he said. "Must of snapped off and fell onto the roof."

"Is there damage?" my mother asked.

"Maybe some dents, nothing too bad," he said. He unzipped the coat, placed it on the back of a chair at the kitchen table, and scratched at his mustache. "Good thing it wasn't the whole tree," he said. "Would of crushed us like a soda can."

He sank down into the couch next to me again, the flashlight still in his hand. "So, what'd I miss?"

The next day, my dad carried our old wooden ladder from the toolshed, leaned it against our trailer, and climbed onto the roof. The orange and yellow sunset reflected the frozen, snow-crusted ground. The raw cold numbed my nose while I stared at the roof—the jagged base of the branch hung over the edge. He yelled down to me that it had missed the furnace vent by only a few inches.

"Could of blown us up," he said. "Or at least caused a pretty bad fire. And you better believe that this baby would burn lickity-split."

He heaved the branch from the trailer roof, and when it cracked onto the ground, I saw that it was no small stick—my dad would need his chain saw to cut it. He climbed back down the ladder, tugged at the bill of his blue McVeytown Volunteer Fire Company hat, and then scanned the snowy yard before looking up at the spot where the branch had broken off the oak tree overhead.

"Hey kiddo, what would you think of living somewhere else?" he asked. "Still by McVeytown but just not in this trailer."

"What's wrong with here?"

He nodded and examined the yard again. "Just could be a lot better, that's all."

My dad had turned thirty the previous November. Though his true passion was the firehouse, he also loved his job cutting glass at Overhead Door—more than once I heard the pride in his voice as he told a friend that he had been the one who cut the glass for new garage doors at TV anchorman Dan Rather's ranch in Texas. But the paychecks barely covered the bills—even I knew he didn't make enough to build a new house. And so, a few weeks after that branch fell, my father did what he thought was the next best thing.

"We're getting a double-wide," he said one night during dinner. "They're bigger than this place, almost like a real house."

My mother carefully laid her fork on the table and looked up from her plate of peas and pork chops. She bit her bottom lip and forced a half smile. "How can we pay for that?"

My dad cracked off a list of ways too complicated for me to understand, though it seemed I wasn't alone when it came to noncomprehension; with each answer he gave, my mother only shook her head and asked more questions. His jaw tightened and his eyes narrowed. When she finally asked where this double-wide would be placed, my dad raised his finger and pointed toward the hole.

"Teena, we already have a foundation practically dug out for it over there," he said.

"The hole? It's full of broken-up cement." My mother shook her head slowly. "You'd have to get somebody to dig it out and then haul all that stuff away. And then on top of that, we'd have to pay for the trailer. We can't afford any of that."

My dad, silent, stared at the checkered oilcloth table cover for a moment. He ran his tongue behind his lips and then scratched at his mustache. Finally, he looked up and nodded. "All right, if you don't want to move, you don't have to. You can leave."

My mother stood, gently pushed her chair against the table, and then walked back the hallway to their bedroom. Her car keys jingled and she opened the back door.

"Teena?" my father called. "Just hear me out."

She closed the door and her footsteps squeaked across the snow. She started her car and drove away.

My dad raised his eyebrows and shook his head as if he had just watched the Steelers lose a game. He continued eating. When he finished his plate, he looked at me.

"You want to live in a new house, right?"

"Yeah," I said, though it made little difference. I just didn't want my father to tell me to leave. I imagined that my dad would buy a double-wide and live next door while my mother and I stayed in the old tin can. We would become like one of those divorced families a few of my friends at school talked about. I'd see my dad on the weekends, when he wasn't busy with the fire company. That was when I usually saw him anyway.

Neither of them spoke when my mother returned home a few hours later. It seemed that for days after that argument, they barely even looked at each other.

But by March, all of the snow had melted and my mother must have warmed to my dad's badgering. Just like with those jokes he told in front of his friends, I didn't understand what happened between them, but it seemed that things were back to normal.

We drove around the midstate for the next several weekends and visited mobile-home dealerships. The lots reminded me of pictures of army barracks—several model trailers sat in rows, their interiors bare and clean. The double-wides we toured seemed like mansions compared to our trailer. They had windows that slid open like in a real house, unlike ours which opened with cranks. They had an actual room for the dining table too; we wouldn't have to eat in a cramped kitchen anymore. Plus, even the smallest bedrooms were double and sometimes triple the size of my current room.

I tugged at my mother's coat as we walked through one of the trailers. "Aren't you excited?" I asked. "These are so much bigger."

She shrugged. "It's still going to come on wheels. It can't be that much better."

It occurred to me that if we did get a double-wide, Lucky would no longer be able to burn his trash in the hole—our new home would sit on top of it. I asked my parents where he would burn his things every Saturday morning, hoping it would be nowhere near us.

"Don't worry," she said. "I don't think he's ever had a problem with that."

My dad turned and walked through the model trailer, past both of us, and didn't say a word.

Five

Overhead Door shut down for vacation during the week of the Fourth of July — it was the only time my dad had off all year until Thanksgiving. On Independence Day, my birthday, my dad drove us to Lewistown for the fireworks display, but first we had to visit Lucky and Helen.

The apartment building they lived in was two stories of red brick, and looked dingy and run-down. All along the street were small houses, their paint peeling or siding falling off, situated so close they seemed to tuck into one another. None of the houses had yards, which seemed impossible to imagine since I spent so much time in ours.

I followed my father up the stairs to their apartment. Behind me, my mother accidentally kicked one of the six-packs of soda that were stacked on every step. My mother had told me that

Helen bought the soda when it was on sale at the store. Over time, the bottles piled up until it looked like she was preparing for some future soda blight when Shasta, RC Cola, and Tab would not be available.

With each step we climbed, the bottled-in heat of the stairwell seemed to rise ten degrees. By the time my father opened the door at the top, I felt as if I could barely breathe. We entered the kitchen, and like always, it smelled of lemony Lysol. Dirty dishes were stacked in the sink.

"Lucky, look who's here," Helen said. She stood in the kitchen and was holding a blue flyswatter. She wore a pastel-colored dress, had her hair up in pink curlers, and her mouth hung agape as though in awe. "Come on, Lucky, it's the birthday boy."

Lucky climbed out of a recliner in the living room and walked across the brown shag carpet and stood next to Helen. He looked like one of those toothpicks he always had in his mouth — tall and thin. Helen was shaped like a football — thick in the belly, wide at the waist.

"Are you having a good birthday?" Helen asked. She spoke in a nasally whine.

"'Course he is," Lucky said. He nodded toward me. "He's a kid. Every day's good for him."

Helen leaned forward, her eyes bulging behind her thick glasses. "Did you see any of your friends today?" she asked. Her wet lips hung open and her tongue slightly protruded from her mouth. My mother always said that one day a fly would buzz into Helen's mouth and she wouldn't even notice.

Before I could answer her first question, she asked another. "Just who are your friends right now?"

"Ben Simpson and Michael Miller are my best friends," I said.

"And what do their parents do?" She shook her head and said, "Well no, wait, do they live in McVeytown?"

"Yeah," I said.

"And do you play sports with them?"

"Sometimes we—"

"I bet they know how to swim already," she said. "I tried to tell your mother that you should be taking swimming lessons this summer. Don't you want to know how to swim?"

"I guess I do."

Helen slowly turned toward my mother and smiled. "Did you hear that? He said that he'd like to know how to swim."

My mother stood with her back against the door, arms crossed. "I already told you that I called the pool," she said, her voice low yet strong. "They said they don't teach swimming lessons to his age group. It wouldn't even do him any good right now. Maybe next summer he'll go."

Helen looked at Lucky. "Why don't you show them to the living room and I'll get some cake ready."

"Show them?" Lucky said. "They've been here before. Unless they went blind and dumb, I'm sure they can find the couch."

Week-old newspapers, opened envelopes, and magazines lay about as if they had simply been left wherever they had first been read, many partially covering dirty plates.

Lucky sank into his orange recliner, its arms spotted with stains. When my dad sat down on the couch, the springs squeaked and clanked; surely if someone of Helen's weight sat on that couch, the entire thing would fall apart.

"Jay, you can sit in the bean bag chair," she said. "I know how much you love that chair."

Helen took special pride in the bean bag chair. Not only was the smiley-face yellow color enough to induce headaches, the chair looked as if it had been sat in by thousands of people. It had the thickness of two pillows, and much of it was held together by swaths of duct tape.

My mother sat on a metal folding chair in the corner. She stared out the small window overlooking a gas station.

"Find a house yet?" Lucky asked. He picked up the latest issue of *Purebred Pigeon* and fingered through the pages.

"Not yet," my dad said. "But we have a few places we'd like to look at this week."

Lucky still stared at the magazine. "Going to be a lot of work. You sure you want to do it?"

"In the end, it'll be good for us."

Lucky nodded and then slapped the magazine onto the floor. He craned his head toward the kitchen. "Where's the cake at, woman? Thought you were bringing it?"

"Give Jay his present," Helen said.

Lucky sighed. He reached next to his chair and tossed a brown paper bag toward me as if throwing a toy to a dog.

"Here you go, boy. You're spoiled, you know that? I never had toys when I was your age. I would have been working."

I opened the bag and pulled out a plastic squirt gun. I recognized it from Jamesway, the local discount chain. When my mother shopped there each Friday night, I spent most of my time in the toy section, examining things like squirt guns. The red pistol

Lucky and Helen bought had been the least expensive on the rack.

"What do you say?" my father said.

"Thanks, Grandma and Pappy," I said.

I had learned to show my grandfather respect, as my father had demanded — he had slapped my mouth when I was very young after I called him Lucky. Though I didn't recall what exactly my father had said, I remembered the sting of his palm against my cheek.

An hour later, my dad parked in a lot in front of Dank's Department Store in downtown Lewistown and we sat in lawn chairs on the bed of his truck.

The Ax Factory, a long, narrow, and dingy building that usually echoed with clanging hammers and hissing machinery, sat oddly quiet next to the parking lot while we waited for the fireworks. The peached haze of dusk slowly faded to black. The parking lot was clustered with families who sat in their cars and pickups and waited for the show.

"You like your new squirt gun?" my dad asked.

"I guess so," I said. "You should get one too. Then we could have a water-gun battle."

"That'd be fun," he said. "But you know, I'm pretty busy right now with the new house."

"Trailer," my mother said.

My dad waved his hand at her. "But it's like a house. This coming week, we're going to Harrisburg and Selinsgrove to look at some. And I heard that the lot in Huntingdon is getting new models at the end of the month. See, if we settle on a trailer by fall, we can excavate the foundation and maybe lay some of the bricks by winter."

He was still talking when the first bang thundered in the sky and echoed against the ridges. Glittering pops of red, white, and blue trailed against the blackened sky. I giggled as the rockets burned high into the sky and then burst. Each blast reverberated into my ears, through my insides. The warm, acrid smell of spent gunpowder drifted into the parking lot like a fog, and for a while it was me and my mom and dad, together in a place and time that felt warm and secure.

On the drive home, my parents reminisced about the day I was born, as they always did after the fireworks. They had worked out the rhythms of the story over the years—switching off for different parts, correcting one another, adding alternative versions of what really happened. Like so much that I later came to know about my family, I guessed that the truth lay somewhere in the middle.

"You weren't due for another week," my mother said. "I had no idea you'd be coming that day. And neither did your father because he wasn't even home."

"Because of what those doctors said," he added.

That afternoon in 1981, my dad hammered the finishing touches on a raft for the annual Juniata River Sojourn—a twenty-five-mile float downriver from nearby Mount Union to Lewistown. A group of men surrounded him in the back parking lot of the firehouse, double-checking that the wooden logs were tied together, that the tarp meant to keep the rafters dry in the water was laced tightly with nylon cord. The men had been out there since morning, drinking water, cracking jokes, and turning pink under the summer sun.

But at home, my mother felt the first of her contractions.

"I thought back to my Lamaze class," she said. "Which your father only ever attended once."

"I was working night shift," he said. "And your classes were in the evening."

She concentrated on breathing, and then, with measured steps, she walked to the telephone in the kitchen, called the firehouse, and left a message for my dad with the station dispatcher. He finally returned home nearly an hour later. Her overnight bag sat on the linoleum in the hallway.

"What took so long?" she asked. They enjoyed acting out the parts and their dialogue.

"Still had some finishing touches to add to the raft," he said. "Figured since I'm not going on the trip now, least I could do was help them finish it."

On the way to the hospital, he stopped at the firehouse once more to tell the dispatcher that he was driving his wife to the Lewistown. My mother sat inside the pickup with the windows rolled down, the thick humidity blanketing the cab.

"Want to make sure they know where I am in case something happens," my father said as he climbed back into the truck.

In the hospital waiting room my father ate Snickers bars and read the latest *Firehouse* magazine. By that night, he held his first, and only, child. In the photos that I've seen from that time, both my parents looked like children themselves. My father, only twenty-three, wore aviator sunglasses in one photo. His hair was thick, combed neatly over his forehead in that mop-top, and a mustache spread over his upper lip. He was thin and in peak physical health. And in the only picture that exists of my mother in the hospital, her face looks flushed and her eyes tired. She was thin too, with straight brown hair and a weary smile. My mother and I stayed at the hospital overnight and the next morning, my dad drove us home.

In the summertime, that trailer sealed the humidity inside like a Ziploc bag. My mother placed box fans in the windows, but they only circulated hot air. On some nights, we slept on the living room floor—it was the only room with enough windows to deflate the heat. The sultry days of summer vacation felt as if they barely passed. Under the lacey ceiling of oak leaves in the backyard, I played in my sandbox, hand-smoothing roads in the sand for my Matchbox cars. Or else I rode the swing on the aluminum jungle gym my father had put together and listened to my Walkman, both birthday presents. I loved oldies music, especially surf and car songs. My dad said that those were the songs he had listened to when he was my age. That week of my birthday, I decided Jan and Dean's "Dead Man's Curve" was the best song I had ever heard. After it ended, I rewound the tape and then listened to it again.

My dad told me that Jan had been in a car crash almost like the one he sang about in the last, eerie verse of the song.

"It was in California," he said. "I remember hearing about it on the radio. He went around a turn one night and bam, ran right into another car parked along the road. Gave him severe brain damage. He could barely talk after that. And, a few years later, Neil Young wrote a song about Jan's brother who died in the crash."

"Does Neil Young sing surf music?"

"No," my dad said. "It's rock and roll. But he's good."

Sometimes when I rode the swing and listened to that Jan and Dean song, I imagined that after the crash at Dead Man's Curve, my father had responded to the accident and had saved Jan's life as surely he had done for dozens of other people.

Exactly what my dad did with the fire company still remained a mystery to me. It seemed a distant world, another life that called him away from my mother and me. There were many times when he had wanted to take me to the firehouse—for chicken and waffle breakfasts, for Santa Claus's annual Sunday afternoon visit, for work-detail nights—but my mother forbade me to go.

"The other guys take their kids," my father pleaded.

"Well, you don't need to take ours," she said. "It's not a place for kids."

And so I searched for clues about my father's secret life. At noon each day, I watched reruns of *CHiPs* on television. My father told me he had loved the cop series when it first aired in the late seventies. When Ponch and Jon raced California freeways on their motorcycles, sirens screaming, lights flashing, I imagined that this was similar to what my father did in his pickup. I asked him about it once and he laughed.

"Not everything is like a television show," he said. "In all the accidents I've been to, I've never seen a car blow up like they do on *CHiPs*. Plus, they always blow up right after Ponch or Jon pulls the victim out."

Still, I built my dad into a hero, based not just on the television shows and movies I watched, but also on how people in McVeytown respected him and his job. It seemed that every time I went somewhere with my dad, someone squatted next to me and said: "Think you want to be a fireman like your dad when you grow up?" It seemed that becoming like him was expected, and a noble goal, as if anything else would be a disappointment. I answered yes even though I didn't understand what it meant—I only hoped that my father would want to see me more.

Six

We had one family outing a year—a day trip to Hershey Park. I anticipated the visits to the park when the first blossoms of spring bubbled to life on the trees. It was the only day of the year when the three of us were together without interruption—no fire company, no Overhead Door, no telephone calls. My father grabbed the radio microphone under the dash of his truck as we drove out of McVeytown that morning.

"Chief Eighty signing off for the day," he said. "I will be out of the area until late tonight."

His pickup lacked a tape deck and the radio had never worked. Instead, I brought my Care Bears portable cassette player and listened to Beach Boys tapes. The single speaker muffled Brian Wilson's vocals and sometimes cracked when the rest of the band sang harmony. But I didn't care. As my father and I sang along with "409" and "Fun Fun Fun," I thought we sounded great.

We passed Mifflintown, Port Royal, and Newport—small towns built along the Juniata River, towns just like McVeytown and Lewistown. Near Newport the Juniata flowed into the Susquehanna, which then snaked next to the highway for miles. My dad drove for two hours straight. Billboards advertising rides at the park appeared near Harrisburg: the Coal Cracker, the Pirate Ship, the Comet, and most impressive of all, the Superdooperlooper, a looped roller-coaster ("The first on the East Coast!") that I had begged to ride with my father ever since I first saw it. Instead, each year I waited with my mother outside the ride's gate and watched him strap into one of the seats. He waved and was then whisked down the track.

"I'd love to take you on it," he always said with regret when the ride finished. "But you're just too short. Maybe next year. It sure was fun, though."

I was sure that I had grown tall enough for it this year. In January, when my class took the President's Physical Fitness Test in gym class, I was the tallest of my class and probably in the whole first grade. I could already jump and grab the monkey bars on the playground during recess—something even few second-graders could do.

"Dad, do you think I can ride the Superdooperlooper with you this year?"

"We'll see," he said. "I hope so. You think you're ready for it? Your mom's still too scared to get on it."

"You couldn't pay me to get on that thing," she said.

Her favorite ride was the Kissing Tower, a nearly 350-foot tower with an escalating and rotating cabin shaped like a Hershey Kiss. Though the panoramic view of Hershey and its surrounding fields looked impressive the first time I had ridden it, the tower had since become the epitome of boring, made even worse by the ride's custom: couples kissed when the cabin reached the top. But when I saw the tower rise on the horizon in a kind of Emerald City–like awe, I wriggled in my seat—that tower always meant that Hershey Park was only minutes away.

Life-size mascots of Hershey bars, Reese's Peanut Butter Cups, and Kisses walked among the crowds inside the park, posed for pictures with families, and waved to the kids. There were water rides, roller-coasters, bumper cars, and arcades. By afternoon, we had covered only half the park and my feet already ached. My parents looked tired and sweaty from the impenetrable heat and humidity.

My father sat down on a bench, moving slowly, as if his joints needed to be oiled. My mother searched for food and drinks. We rested a few minutes, listening to the distant scream of riders plummeting down hills on roller-coasters. The sweet smell of cotton candy and chlorine-soaked water mixed in the air. Dad removed his hat and wiped his forehead on the sleeve of his shirt. My mother walked back from one of the food vendors with a tray of hot dogs and Cokes. She sat next to my father and handed me a drink. Then she paused and studied his flushed face.

"What's wrong? Do you want some water? You don't look so good."

He shook his head and sighed. "I just feel wiped out all of a sudden."

She patted his back, concerned, and offered him a Coke. It was the first time I had ever seen him worn out like this, especially on our outing at Hershey Park. Usually he marched over the paved paths with vigor, delighting in the rides almost as much I did.

We sat a few minutes longer. Sweat beaded down my father's forehead, and his eyes looked glassy and bloodshot.

Finally, he cleared his throat and stood. "Ready to get back at it?"

"You sure you feel okay?" my mother asked.

He smiled and rolled his eyes. "I'll be fine. Besides, we only get here one day a year. Might as well make the most of it."

We escaped more than just the fire company during our little vacation—for that one day there was no mention of Helen and Lucky. Though my father had never said so outright, I sensed that his family had never taken a vacation when he was a child. He never spoke of good times or having fun with his family—it was as if those times were secret.

One time I asked if Lucky ever played catch with my father or his brothers. "Nope," my dad said but he offered no explanation why, or about how it made him feel. I guessed that it was because Lucky worked a lot on construction projects, seasonal work with few jobs during the winter months.

I wondered if my dad felt neglected like me. One time, while my father sat on the living room floor playing Chutes and Ladders with me, the alarm codes sounded on his pager. He leaped up from the game, kicked the board and its plastic pieces into the air, and dashed for his bunker boots in the bedroom. At over six feet tall, my dad looked like a giant inside our tiny trailer. When he jumped up that day, adrenaline lifted him off the ground so high that he smashed his head on a light mounted in the hallway ceiling. Shards of glass sprinkled down onto the linoleum, but he didn't stop for a second; he just ran out the door. I cried throughout the night, wanting him back home, sitting on the floor with me.

But at Hershey Park I had him all to myself, even if it was for just a day. And my father seemed to love it. We threw kernels of corn into some of the park's streams and watched fat ducks peck at the water. He laughed with me.

At dusk, we finally came to the Superdooperlooper. The roaring cars breezed past overhead and passengers screamed. I had seen boys in the park not much older than I was wearing I SURVIVED THE SUPERDOOPERLOOPER! T-shirts.

"Can we get on it, Dad?" I tugged on his hand. "I know I can do it this year."

"I don't know, Shorty," he said. "Unless you sprout about two inches in the next minute, I don't think you can."

"Come on, Dad, can't I get on?"

My mother smiled and shrugged. "This is all he talked about last week when you were at work."

My dad squeezed my hand. "Maybe next year. You'll grow by then."

"You promise?"

"Promise," he said. He walked through the gate and toward stairs leading to the boarding area. He turned and held his hand over his chest. "We'll ride it together next year, scout's honor."

I felt a pang of sadness, reminded of what it would be like the rest of the year, when I would be left alone when he went to the firehouse.

Our final ride of the day had always been the Giant Wheel, a Ferris wheel with round, cagelike seats instead of benches. We ascended into a sky now matted with the deep purples and blues of the approaching night. Hershey Park spread out below us, a switchboard of twinkling lights. Across the maze of food stands and rides, the Kissing Tower glimmered like a monument.

Leaving the park hurt worse than the year-long wait to return. I grabbed my father's wrist and looked at his watch, begging not to leave—we still had fifteen minutes, enough time for one more ride. As we walked toward my father's truck, my feet felt sore. Other families walked next to us—exhausted parents yelled at their screaming children and told them that the park was closing. My father wobbled a bit, the same as he'd done sometimes when he returned from a fire.

"Hey, Dad, did you ever come here when you were a kid?"

"Nope," he said.

"Pappy Varner never took you?"

"We never went on vacation," my father said. "But after I graduated high school, I went to Disney World with a friend of mine."

"Really? You think we could go there some time?"

"We should," he said. "One of these days, sure."

When he climbed into his truck, he sighed and waited a moment to turn the key. On the ride home, I didn't play any Beach Boys songs. We sat in silence, my head resting against my mother's arm. I was already dreaming of next year's trip, praying I would grow just a few more inches so that I could ride the Superdooperlooper.

When we drove back through McVeytown, my dad picked up his radio microphone.

"Chief Eighty, signing back in."

Seven

Lucky continued his Saturday morning fires throughout that summer and started bringing a friend along with him. The man had an unkempt beard, greasy hair, and always wore jeans that hung low around his waist, exposing his butt.

"Mom, who's that guy with Lucky?" I asked the first time he showed up. "He looks like one of those guys we see hitchhiking along the highway."

My mother walked to the living room window and looked out. Without saying a word, she turned and locked the front door. Then she crossed the trailer and locked the back. She had never done this before. Something was wrong.

"Mom, who is he?"

"His name is Ricky Trutt," she said. "And you are not to go outside when he's here. Do you understand me?"

"I don't go out anyway."

She knelt next to me and placed her hands on my shoulders. "Do not go outside when he's here. Do you understand?"

"Okay," I said, even though I wondered why.

Every Friday night we went to Lewistown for groceries. Small shops lined Valley Street, the main street through Lewistown: Kay's Sporting Goods, Video Vendor, Foss's Jewelers, and C. G. Murphy's, which still had a lunch counter. Families and couples walked the streets at dusk and window-shopped. Teenagers cruised past the cannons perched on the lawn of the Civil War–themed town square. While my mother shopped for groceries at the Giant Store, my father sometimes took me along with him for a visit to the Coleman House, the hotel Lucky and Helen owned.

The building sat on that town square and dated back to the late 1800s, when Lewistown had begun to transform into a tidy little city. Once, it had been a popular and respectable place. A man named Harry Gardiner, who my father said was called the Human Fly, had as a publicity stunt climbed the outside of the seven-story hotel in the 1920s. In the years since then, the quality and care had declined. By the time my grandparents purchased it for next to nothing, the hotel housed Lewistown's riffraff—the low cost of rooms was cheaper than renting an apartment. Most of the residents were men soaked in cheap liquor and dressed in stained clothing. Many were also Lucky's friends.

"Grandma and Pappy will be glad to see you," my dad said as he opened the glass door to the building's lobby. "I bet Grandma will even give you some candy."

"No, Dad, please no candy. Last time it was terrible."

At Halloween the year before, my dad had painstakingly painted my face in a clown disguise and insisted on taking me to the hotel to show his parents. As usual, Helen cooed and hawed; Lucky, though, propped his feet on the counter and stared at the opposite wall. The Reese's Peanut Butter Cups Helen gave me that day looked like they were covered with cataracts, misshapen and hazed over with the kind of whiteness teachers at school warned us not to eat. I was certain that the candy in that display case near the front hotel's desk hadn't been freshened since last Halloween.

A television in the lobby blasted *Wheel of Fortune.* Three grizzled men sat on couches and stared in silence at the screen. The upholstery was ripped in spots, revealing yellow foam. The tiled floor had probably been white at one time; it now resembled the crusted bug shield on the hood of my father's truck.

Helen, wearing a flower-print dress, stood behind the display case and wrote inside a log book next to the cash register. She looked up and smiled.

"Oh Lucky, look who's here," she said. "It's Jay and Denton."

Lucky sat in a recliner behind the counter reading *National Geographic.* He stood and placed the magazine on the seat of the chair.

"You ever read *National Geographic,* boy? You should. It'd make you smart."

"Come on back here and give your grandma a big hug," Helen said. She opened the flimsy particle board gate to let me behind the counter. "You want some candy?"

"He doesn't need any," my dad said. I squeezed his wrist and smiled up at him — if I held on to him, perhaps I wouldn't be forced behind the desk for that dreadful hug. The scent of Helen's cheap perfume always seemed to cling to my clothes.

"Well, guess what?" my dad said. He smiled and paused, letting the tension build. "We found a house."

Lucky tongued at his toothpick. "Did you now?"

"Looks like we'll be moving in by March or April," my dad said.

"Oh Lucky, can you believe it?" Helen said. She turned to Lucky and smiled. "A new house. I can't wait to see it. How big is it? Does it have a dining room? You should at least have a dining room. And you're still going to build a basement, right?"

My dad nodded and explained that the double-wide was twice the size of our current trailer. He'd already made the calls to contractors for estimates on a basement.

"And you're still putting it where our old house used to be?" Lucky asked. He flicked the toothpick into a trash can behind the counter. "Lot of good memories there."

"Remember my ring, Lucky?" Helen asked. She turned to me, her mouth loose and smiling. "The first wedding ring your grandfather bought me, I took it off to wash dishes and I put it on the windowsill. And wouldn't you know, it fell out the window and onto the ground. I never found it after that." She scratched at her knee and lifted the purple dress up so high that it exposed a thick, panty-hosed thigh. I'd noticed this habit before — she often pulled up her dress, exposed her legs, and sometimes caressed her thighs.

"I looked high and low for that ring," Lucky said. "I didn't want to lose it."

A lost treasure hunt flashed in my mind, a Saturday spent climbing over those busted concrete slabs, gliding a metal detector over the ground, all in search of that lost diamond ring.

"So it's still there?" I asked. "Do you think it might still be worth something?"

" 'Course it's worth something, boy," Lucky said. "It's a diamond. You think they're free? In Africa, little boys like you get told to go into mines to dig them out. And if they don't dig in the mines, they get sold to people who'll make them behave."

My dad and his parents chatted for a few minutes about the trailer and about the fire company. Lucky listened with a blank stare while Helen nodded and smiled. When Lucky asked my father to look at a window in one of the rooms upstairs, I begged him to take me along with him. The only remotely fun part about visiting the hotel was riding the elevator—an old-time contraption with a lever that had no doubt once been run by a bellhop. My father pulled the latticed metal gate across the elevator's doorway and then yanked the lever. After a jerk, the cables grinded and we rose to the third floor, where my dad stepped out and told me to wait inside the elevator. He walked down the hallway and went into a room. The mud brown carpet looked polka-dotted with black stains. The entire place smelled of turpentine and dirty socks. After a few minutes, my dad came out of the room and we descended back to the lobby.

"Fixed it," my dad said. "The spring inside was busted. I left the window open. Stunk pretty bad in there."

Lucky nodded and thanked him. He eased back into his

recliner again, the *National Geographic* in his hand. "I think Ricky Trutt and I might be up again soon. Got some old mattresses I want to burn up."

My father dug both hands into his pockets. "Didn't I tell you what Teena said about Ricky?"

Lucky stared back, unblinking and angry. "You told me. And you can tell her that it's my ground. I can do what I want on my ground."

"Dad, come on," my father said. "I'll help you burn them. He doesn't need to come along."

"If she doesn't like him, then you tell her to leave," Lucky said. "I don't tell her who she can talk to. Ricky's coming and that's all there is to it."

My dad didn't speak. The sound of *Jeopardy!* spilled over the lobby. He glanced at his watch and said that we should leave. He took my hand and we walked out of the hotel. I wondered what my mother had said about Ricky Trutt and just why she always locked the doors when he came around.

My father stared blankly out the windshield as he drove.

"Dad, what happened to that house near our trailer?" I asked.

"Which house?"

"Your old house, when you were a kid," I said. "The one we're going to put the trailer on?"

He held his stare for a moment and cleared his throat. "You know, that's funny. It burned down." His voice softened. He tapped his fingers on the steering wheel as if nervous. "I remember losing all my toys. Slot cars, Rock'em Sock'em Robots, Lincoln Logs, and LEGOS. Board games too, like Candy Land and Chutes and Ladders."

These were the same toys that he had bought me for Christmases and birthdays. If he never played with them as a child, I wondered why he never wanted to play with me now.

"All the photos burned up too," he said. "I don't even have any pictures of me when I was your age."

"How did it catch on fire?" I asked.

"Just an accident," he said sharply. "It was an accident. That's why you should always be careful with matches and things like that. Fire is dangerous."

Lucky stopped his weekly fires at the hole—it would soon be excavated with backhoes, and then bricklayers would arrive to lay the cinder-block foundation. One Saturday night at the end of August, my mother and I walked around the heavy, iron I beams that sat next to the hole. I begged her to watch me balance myself on the beams like a tightrope walker. My dad promised to come outside and play Wiffle ball with me once he got off the phone. Probably talking to one of his friends in the fire company, I thought.

The back screen door on the trailer slammed shut and he walked across the driveway and onto the dirt. He glanced at my mother, sighed, and then looked toward the horizon. He often did this when nervous, as if he wished he were following the sunset to somewhere else. He jingled change in his pockets.

"That was my mother on the phone," he said. "Dad's on his way up here to burn some things from the hotel."

"Some things?" my mother said. "You said he wasn't coming back."

My father tugged the bill of his hat, rubbed his neck, and said, "It's his ground. I can't tell him not to."

She crossed her arms and looked toward the highway. "Well, it's too late now. Here he comes."

Lucky's pickup crowned the hill, and as he slowed, I saw that the bed was piled with mattresses. The trailer hitched to the back of his truck was also filled with them. Another truck followed behind. I instantly recognized the driver, who had a scraggly brown beard and a hollow face, as Ricky Trutt. His truck was also piled high with mattresses.

"Go inside," my mother told me. "I'll be there in a minute."

I ran across the yard and up the porch steps. I turned and saw the trucks drive over the lawn, past my jungle gym and the tool shed, and then stop. They had parked next to the cement floor left over from where the workshop had once stood.

When my mother came inside, she locked the door behind her. We huddled around the kitchen window and watched.

My dad climbed onto the back of the truck and grabbed one end of a mattress, Lucky grabbed the other. Together, they swung the thing back and forth and finally tossed it onto the ground. They continued until both trucks and trailers were empty. My father talked with Lucky and Ricky for a few moments. Then he walked across the yard, unlocked the door, and came inside. My mother sat on a chair at the kitchen table. When my dad crossed his arms, leaned against the wall, and looked toward her, she continued to stare out the window.

"What?" he asked.

"What are they doing?" she asked. "It's almost dark."

"He's just burning some old mattresses from the hotel."

"I thought you told him not to bring Ricky Trutt here anymore." Her words came slow yet forceful, as if holding back a scream.

My father shrugged and said, "Dad needed the help."

"He needs help," my mother said. She turned from the window and looked at my father. "He's sick. They're both sick. And did you have to help them? They shouldn't let that man have matches. It's illegal for murderers to have guns."

"What do you mean?" He laughed and shook his head. I could tell that he wanted her to drop the issue.

"You threw those mattresses off the truck with them."

"My father can't do things like that anymore," he said. "Do you want him to have a heart attack?"

"How dare he keep coming here with that creep, in front of his grandson no less." She stood, pressed a hand against her cheek, and said, "You know why Lucky comes here, Denton?"

My father pointed at her. "Don't you say it."

"Why? You don't want your son to hear it?"

"Hear what?" I asked.

My dad squinted at my mother and clenched his jaw. He marched toward the door again, stomping his feet so hard that I thought they were going to pound right through the floor of the kitchen. He slammed the door and then walked back across the yard toward my grandfather. My mother and I continued watching out the kitchen window.

Lucky and Trutt circled the mattresses and splashed them with gasoline. Then, just as he had done for those Saturday morning blazes, Lucky poured a small trail through the grass and away from the mattresses. He struck a match and dropped it onto the ground. He and Trutt hustled backward and watched the flames erupt. Air hissed and the crackling roar sounded like a jet engine. A ginger-colored lambency spread in ripples across the yard and leaked through the windows of our trailer. That glow from the flames swirled on the ceiling, bounced off the walls, and the trailer felt submerged in some kind of intangible hell.

My mother and I stepped onto the porch and watched the roaring fire. I felt the warmth of the flames press against my face. Heat devils shimmered in the air and smoke clouded up into the blackening evening sky. The inferno was perhaps thirty yards away from us, and my grandfather and his friend stood beside it, their postures relaxed as though watching a fireworks display. The smell of smoke thickened the air. I had never seen anything like it, and my heart beat hard inside my chest in fear. My grandfather had done this, I thought.

My dad walked onto the porch and stood next to my mother and me. Sweat beads sparkled on his forehead.

"Can't you make them put it out, Dad?" I looked up at my father but his eyes were fixed on the fire. I tugged at his jeans and asked again.

"It's his land," he said. He shook his head and looked to the ground. "I can't stop him."

"But you're the fire chief," I said. "What if it spreads into the fields? What if it comes toward the house?" Vast fields of fire spread through my imagination—helicopters hovered in the sky, dropping bursts of water onto the scene, and men with axes raced toward the flames. My father commanded all of them like a general in battle.

"I don't know," my dad finally said. "I don't know."

Part Two

Eight

I grab a pen and a notebook off my desk as elongated beeps from the scanner alarm pierce the newsroom's mid-evening silence. I turn up the volume and listen. It is early October, and though I have worked at the *Sentinel* for more than a month, I have yet to go out on a fire call. The beeps stop and I wait for the dispatcher to break the brief fuzz of silence.

"Structure fire," the voice says. His voice sounds calm and routine. "Four twenty-one Back Mountain Road, Allensville. Neighbor reports flames in the upstairs with possible entrapment."

Entrapment is all I need to hear—that means reporters go no matter what.

"Lorrie, get the camera," I yell. "We got a fire."

The alarm codes blast again. I grab my laminated press pass and head out. Lorrie already leans against a cubicle at the end of the newsroom, camera bags slung over each shoulder. She adjusts her glasses and raises her eyebrows. "So where we going?"

Lorrie is in her midfifties and previously worked as a paramedic in inner-city Pittsburgh, then as a paralegal, but when she throws her camera bags onto the floor of my car and tells me to hurry up, I wonder how she could have ever been anything other than a newspaper photographer.

We speed through the darkness and toward the fire. I stomp the gas pedal and my Ford Tempo bucks over potholed dips and veers tightly around sharp, sudden bends. We double the posted speed limit of thirty-five miles per hour on the narrow, back-country road. Black and white spots of Holstein cattle blur in the periphery of my high-beamed lights. The lit windows of old stone farmhouses glow like smudges of yellow on night's dark canvas. I speed past signs for dairy farms and churches, and I drive over clumps of manure from horses that pulled Amish buggies.

Anxiety flutters my brain and cramps my stomach. My fingers grip the steering wheel tightly and my knuckles ache. This is my initiation, my entry into the ring of fire that has held my family in thrall for years. I have dreaded my first fire for more than the simple threat of unburied memories; it is the rush that I fear too. I squeeze the steering wheel harder and stare at the road ahead.

One month earlier, on a Saturday in early September, I walked toward Jimmy's Pizza, a two-story house converted into a restaurant located on McVeytown's tiny square, a place I went most Saturdays for lunch with my three cousins.

In McVeytown, everyone already knew me because of my father, but my byline in the local newspaper turned me into a small-town celebrity. A man I didn't even know walked past me on the street and said, "Nice work." The driver of a passing car waved and beeped his horn. I thought back to those evenings when I rode into McVeytown with my father, how everyone had either waved or said hello to him. It seemed kind of like the same thing, except I know that I'm not like my dad—I'm supposed to write about men like him.

Though my first few stories were routine—a DNA kit used to identify kidnapped children, Lewistown borough council meetings, Mifflin County school board meetings—many people read them. Anytime I deposited my paycheck at the bank or used my debit card, the person behind the counter glanced at my name and smiled.

"Are you the same Jay Varner who writes for the newspaper?"

That Saturday, I walked into Jimmy's and smelled the spaghetti sauce. The Penn State football pregame show blasted on the radio, the announcers running down the list of Nittany Lions.

"There's Walter Winchell," my cousin Trevor said when I sat down in the corner booth next to my other cousins, Paul and David. "Watch out, he might write a story about us."

I told them the rumors and gossip we couldn't print: which local officials are jerks or drunks, how bad the local heroin problem really is. I found out quickly that this is one of the greatest perks of a newsroom, what every reporter thrives on — access to the behind-the-scenes details, glimpses of true personalities, knowing everything before others read it in the newspaper.

"So what else they got you writing?" Paul asked.

"We're doing a weekly feature on small towns," I said.

"Think McVeytown will be in there?" Trevor asked. His question came out more as a statement than as a question thanks to his Pennsylvania accent.

"I'm the one writing it." I smiled and looked toward the front of the restaurant. "And I can tell you the first place I'm going to start — right there with that man at the counter."

Jimmy Cooper, the owner of the restaurant and perhaps the most famous man in McVeytown, stood behind the register and handed cash back to a customer. He wore a maroon polo shirt embroidered with his restaurant's logo — a smiling, mustached man flipping a pizza. He chatted with the customer for a few moments and laughed.

"Don't tell Jimmy about it," I said. "It's still a month off and I want it to be a surprise. You know he'll get a kick out of it."

When we finished eating, I excused myself and stepped outside for a cigarette.

"Stick that cigarette up your ass," Jimmy said as he walked out of the restaurant's back door. "It'll do you more good."

"It's my job," I said. "Stresses me out."

"It's Saturday and I'm the one who's working. Besides, what the hell do you do that's so important?"

"I'm writing for the paper now."

He lowered his palm to his crotch and jerked his hand as

though masturbating. He smiled, patted my shoulder, and walked toward his new Lexus parked on the street.

Jimmy Cooper reminded me of my father in a lot of ways. Everyone loved talking to him because he always had a joke or a smile. If someone in McVeytown dealt with a tragedy, like losing their house in a fire or struggling to pay medical bills for their sick child, Jimmy always sat a jar on the counter next to the cash register for donations. He had a way of making his customers and friends feel good about life. None of us knew it was all an act.

"You have any advice for me?" I ask Lorrie, an attempt to keep my mind off of what is coming. "I haven't been to one of these yet."

The most important thing, Lorrie says, is to stay out of the way of the fire crews. The last thing they want to deal with is a nosy reporter who could slow them down. Never park near fire hydrants, never drive over hoses, and never ask questions until they have started to put away their gear. Ask for the chief in command, she says, because most of the other guys will have simply done what they were ordered. And write down the names of all fire companies involved—it's important to make sure all the crews are credited in the article.

Sweat beads down my forehead. My arms tremble. On the last straight stretch into Allensville, where cornfields and pastures flank the road, my speedometer creeps toward eighty. After we crest a hill outside town, red and blue strobe lights flash in quick bursts at the end of town. Fire trucks, ambulances, and police cruisers clog the road. I slow the car, pull into the parking lot of a Mennonite church, and grab my notepad off the floor. Lorrie is out of the car before I even kill the engine, the camera bags slung over her shoulders.

"Come on," she says. She stops and waits for me, her hands on her waist. "Remember what I told you."

"I can't find my press pass."

She laughs and holds up her black camera bags. "You think they're going to ask any questions when they see these puppies? Besides, they all know me."

I close the door and jog to catch up with her. The chilly breeze stings my face. Smoke, or rather its stale and blistered scent, wafts in the night air. We walk past hissing pink flares that burn bright as a welder's torch. The churn of generators and the growl of idling fire engines fill what would otherwise be a quiet night in Allensville. The townspeople line their front yards, cross their arms, and watch the scene as if it were the annual Independence Day parade.

Lorrie and I walk toward the smoke. Hoses protrude from fire engines like tentacles; fine jets of mist spew from metal adapters that connect them. Water puddles on the narrow street and in the grass of front yards. We trail the fire hose along a broken sidewalk that takes us past more fire engines and ambulances that line a side street. Footsteps clump behind me. I turn just in time to sidestep a rushing fireman—his helmet on, face shield down—holding a chain saw. I stand transfixed by the constant twinkles of strobe lights and then the rush of still more firemen and a few paramedics. I fumble with my notebook, flip open to a clean page, and scribble the names of companies I see on the sides of the fire trucks: Belleville, Allensville, Fame, Brooklyn, Burnham, and the McVeytown Volunteer Fire Company. If I get their names wrong, I know that the prideful firefighters won't soon forgive me.

The Monday after I ate at Jimmy's Pizza with my cousins, I typed an obituary at my desk in the newsroom and monitored the police and fire calls that crackled from the scanner. Eight out of ten were advanced life-support calls for ambulances — chest pains, shortness of breath, or dizziness. In the three weeks since I started working for the paper, I had written maybe a half-dozen obits for suicides. Suicide seemed just as common as cancer in the area. Most were middle-aged men who had recently lost their jobs.

At around four in the afternoon I heard the dispatch for a gunshot victim. I turned up the volume to listen — guns usually meant violence, crime, front-page news. Instead, the dispatcher informed the ambulance crew en route to the scene that the victim, who had been found in the basement by his father, was clutching a shotgun and not breathing. The dispatchers never gave out names, only addresses, and the one I heard meant nothing to me.

"What's going on?" a reporter sitting next to me asked.

"Suicide," I said. "Another one."

I turned down the volume and continued to write an obituary for someone who had overdosed on heroin.

It was late when I returned home that night, and I crept into my bedroom, careful not to wake my mother.

"Are you just now getting back?" she asked from across the hall. Her voice was sharp and clear. I could tell that she hadn't been asleep.

"Yeah," I said.

She was quiet for a moment. "Did you hear what happened?"

"What?" I stood in her doorway while a dozen awful things raced through my mind. My heart felt like it might crack through my ribs.

"You didn't hear?" she asked. Her voice sounded mournful, as though she pitied me for what I was about to hear. "Jimmy Cooper shot himself. I thought you'd have heard it at work."

Jimmy was the gunshot victim, the one in the basement, clutching a shotgun. I shuddered, hoping the dispatcher's voice would get out of my head.

"I did hear it," I said. "It was on the scanner. Is he okay?"

She waited and finally said, "Jay, he died."

I remembered joking with Jimmy just a few days earlier. He had seemed like his usual self. An image flashed through my head—Jimmy hugging a shotgun, his toe on the trigger. For a moment, I think that none of this could have possibly happened—it didn't make sense. Everyone loved Jimmy.

I called my cousin Trevor, but neither of us could really talk—the conversation was more silence and sighs than anything else. When I hung up the phone, I felt as if the blood had been drained from my body.

That night, the darkness seemed to drag on forever—I snapped awake, lunging upright and gasping, as though a gunshot shattered the early morning silence. By the time the bruised light of dawn leaked through my curtains, I dreamed that Jimmy's ghost stood in my bedroom. He wore a Pittsburgh Pirates T-shirt and gray gym shorts. He scratched at his brown mustache and laughed. When I woke the final time, full-blown daylight seeped into my bedroom. I lay still for a moment and decided that I couldn't write this obit; I couldn't write any story about Jimmy, not the one I'd planned and certainly not this one.

The once-white borders of two windows on the top floor of the house are now soot-black from the smoke. A roof juts over the front porch. Floodlights blast a hyperbright glow over the scene. It feels like something from a movie set. Firefighters climb a ladder onto the porch roof and spray bursts of water through two windows and onto whatever smolders inside. A hole about the size of a bathtub has burned through the roof and a weak swell of smoke escapes.

The family clusters under a looming oak tree ten yards from their damaged home. The father crosses his arms defiantly, as though already mapping a plan to repair the house; the mother holds a crying baby. They speak with a fireman who gestures with his hands and points at the house. A white helmet, just like the one my father wore, caps the man's head, and I think immediately of my father's old helmet that sits in a box in our basement. Every now and then I pull it out and trace my fingers over the reflective trim that reads CHIEF 80, and then I crown my head with the heavy helmet. I feel my father's presence. It doesn't matter that I can't see the chief's face—his tall, steady frame is enough to remind me of my father, and I wonder how many times he stood in that same position.

Lorrie weaves between firemen and steps over the now deflated hoses. When she snaps pictures of the cleanup operation, the bulb flashes a second of white light on the backs of firemen.

I walk up to a man standing on the street. He glances at my notebook and squints.

"Sir, I'm a reporter with the *Sentinel*," I say. "Did you see anything that happened?"

"Yep." He still holds his stare. "But I ain't talking to you. Don't want my name in the paper."

I shake my head. "I don't even have to use your name. I just wondered what the fire looked like?"

"I ain't saying nothing to you." He looks back at the house.

I nod and move a few paces down the street, where a couple stands. They turn, see me, and walk away. Great. I can't even interview witnesses—how am I going to interview the firemen?

As the firemen roll up hoses and remove their jackets, I search for someone to question. I look back for the chief, who spoke with the family before, but he is gone. I scribble in my notebook in an attempt to look busy, too timid to ask any of the firemen to point me in the right direction. While I write, Lorrie taps me on the shoulder and smiles.

"Down there's the family," Lorrie says. "You could ask them what happened."

The family still clusters in the front yard. They wear black and for the first time I realize that they are Mennonite.

"Would you want some reporter asking you how you felt in a situation like this?" I ask.

"Well, no." Lorrie frowns—we both know this is a necessary part of the job. After a few moments, she slowly nods. "Come on, let's get the chief for you."

My shoes squish as I walk, soaked from the runoff of the hoses. We pass some firemen who light cigarettes and talk about their families. The sting of smoke lingers in the air and tears my eyes. Finally, we come to a fifty-ish man with a gentle hand-shake. He has the wrinkled skin of someone who has worked outside his entire life.

I ask him to give me the details of the fire. I learn it started when a candle in the upstairs bathroom brushed against a curtain.

"What about the report of entrapment?"

"The neighbor said that there were children living here," he says. "He didn't know if they'd made it out or not, so the dispatcher said possible entrapment. Better to be safe than sorry."

He grins and nods. I write all of it down.

Satisfied that I have enough information for a story, I feel my trembling begin to stop, my breath and heart slow. I hold on to my notebook with one hand, shake loose a cigarette from a pack of Camel Lights with another, and light up. I listen as Lorrie chats with the fire chief for a minute more. As she walks away, I nod to the chief.

"Thanks again," I say. "Oh, I don't think I introduced myself. Jay Varner. I'm covering the fire beat for the paper now."

He smiles, extends his hand, and says, "Bob Barger."

As I reach to shake, I realize that I'm still holding the burn-ing cigarette. "Sorry," I said, and switch the cigarette to my left hand. "You probably don't need a burn from me."

"Yeah, I've got enough scars." He smiles. "Varner? Where you from?"

"McVeytown."

"You related to Denton?"

"He was my dad."

"He was a good man," he says. "I remember seeing him at a lot of things like this. It's a shame, what cancer did to him and all." He glances at the cigarette and then at me, a silent admoni-tion that I should know better.

"Well Jay, I'm glad to know you're the one who'll be writing this up," he says. "I think your dad would have liked that."

The Saturday after Jimmy Cooper killed himself, Trevor and I talked late into the night. My cousin still lived with his parents in Mattawana, a sleepy little cluster of houses across the river from McVeytown. We smoked cigarettes on the front porch and recounted Jimmy's last days, pouring through what information we had, trying to piece together the mystery of his death, just as many of us had done at his funeral. Our conversation soon expanded to include the death of Lewistown. We talked about all the jobs that had been lost, all the stores and factories that had closed.

Nearly 5 percent of the town's population had lost work in the past few months. First, Lear Corp. shut down its factory, firing 308 employees who once manufactured automotive carpeting.

The same month, Standard Steel, a company founded in 1795, closed its ring mill which produced locomotive wheels. The company continued to operate its Lewistown plant but without the 109 workers who lost their jobs. When the Ax Factory in downtown Lewistown closed, forty-nine people—the only remnants of a thriving past when seven times that number had been employed there—all lost their jobs.

The town's slide reached beyond just the economy. After I graduated from high school, Lewistown became known for its drug epidemic, the worst in Pennsylvania outside of Philadelphia and Pittsburgh. In 2001, MSNBC devoted much of a two-hour exposé called "America's New Heroin Epidemic: Along Comes the Horse" to the situation in Lewistown. Anchorman Forrest Sawyer stood in front of the town square decorated with cannons and an American flag, a pastiche on the picturesque small town in twilight, and noted how drug use had inexplicably soared.

At Lewistown's municipal building, where the borough council meets twice a month, a faded, off-white banner hung on the inside wall: LEWISTOWN—ALL-AMERICAN CITY, 1973. At the meetings I covered, the borough council talked about the drug problem as they had been doing for years. A handful of citizens complained to the council and the town's police chief about drug deals that were going down in their neighborhoods, on their streets.

"Did you know that in nineteen sevnty-three, Lewistown was named an All-American City?" I asked Trevor. "Makes you wonder just what in the hell happened? Feels like everything is dying."

"Yeah," Trevor said. "But I love this town."

"It's my hometown, but it's not my home anymore," I said. "The town—McVeytown, Lewistown, whatever—it's lost too much."

We sat in silence for a moment, and listened to a freight train beat over the railroad tracks along the river. The sound was both lonely and cold, as if the rest of the world couldn't pass through Mifflin County fast enough.

"Now, it seems like there's nothing here," I said. "It's like Bruce says, 'Main Street's whitewashed windows and vacant stores.'"

Trevor stared off into the night sky and nodded. "Then you know what you have to do," he said. "You have to get out. And I don't blame you."

In the midmorning hours, I finally left for home. As I drove down the hill from Trevor's house, I looked across the Juniata River at the fiery blue, yellow, and white lights of McVeytown. Each light appeared as solitary and lost as the next, yet all of them together seemed to weave a circuit board of grief. I wondered what had happened to this town, to Mifflin County. I had watched stores close, seen neighbors come and go, and both hated and loved these streets through the years. But that was then. The area seemed to hold more of my past than future.

I pulled up to the flashing red light in McVeytown, the town's only stoplight, and looked across the street. Jimmy's Pizza sat in the dark. In the past week, every time I drove through McVeytown, I thought of Jimmy standing behind the counter, his flour-covered hands tossing pizza dough.

And, each time I passed the McVeytown Volunteer Fire Company on my way home from the newspaper, I still thought of my father. Though it didn't make any sense, I felt like in losing Jimmy, I had lost another part of my father.

Lorrie and I say little on the drive back to the newsroom. The adrenaline that had flared through my blood is now drained from my body and I feel exhausted. Still, I can't get over the thrill of it, the bolt of excitement and fear I had felt on the way there. The house could have been fully engulfed, flames licking at the black night sky, and there I would have been in the center of it all.

"I never realized what they did," I tell Lorrie. We are five minutes away from the office. Deadline is only a half hour away, but I know Elizabeth is waiting for the story and will hold up the press run.

"What who did?" Lorrie asks.

"Firemen," I say. "My dad was a fireman. I hated him for a lot of years because he was always leaving when he got a call. But I never thought of all the other people he was with. People like that family back there. If there had been a kid trapped in that house, he'd have gone in."

Lorrie nods. "Any one of those men would have gone in."

"I know. I just feel a little guilty all of a sudden. Maybe I shouldn't have held it against him."

I wonder if my dad ever saved someone's life as a fireman. Or if he lived with the guilt of not being able to charge into a burning house, and instead watched someone die.

"Why did your dad become a fireman?" Lorrie asks.

I think a moment. "When he was a kid, his house burned down."

Lorrie sits in silence the rest of the way back to the newsroom. After I finish writing the story, I step outside for a cigarette. I stand alone in the cool night air and feel confident that I have written a good article. But boredom dulls the satisfaction. The newsroom seems so still and deadening. Tonight has offered the only rush of happiness I have felt since Jimmy died. I yearn for another fire, wonder when the scanner will blast out those alarm codes again. How fast can I drive to the next one, how soon can I get there? A spark has been lit inside me, the same one that had driven my father away from me while he was alive, and kept him there after he was dead. But I wonder if perhaps I am finally starting to understand him.

Nine

Our yard looked like a dump and my mother hated it.

A bulldozer pushed down the old cement walls where Lucky had stored his pigeons—he had shown up one day at the end of August and moved the birds. A backhoe then excavated the hole, scooping dirt, cement, and metal onto a dump truck, which then transplanted the junk across our yard and piled it onto the ruins of the house. What resulted looked like a mountain of rubbish: dirt, rusted metal piping, busted cinder blocks, and chunks of cement.

One evening, not long after the dig was finished, my parents and I walked around the pile of debris as if we were surveyors. Dusk had turned damp and wet with the approach of fall. Fog smoked over the fields. In our backyard, tree branches sagged from the weight of ripening red apples.

The smell of honeysuckle wafted in the breeze, mixing with the wet scent of dirt and clay. I scanned the pile for a glint or flash, hoping that Helen's diamond ring might have been unearthed.

My father appraised the pile as he walked. He held out his hand toward the dirt and cement as if it were an award on a game show. "Looking pretty good, don't you think? Give the dirt a few weeks to settle and I think it'll be fine."

My mother stopped, leaned against one of the English walnut trees, and crossed her arms. "It's an eyesore. It looks like we live in a construction site."

"Beats paying to have it hauled off somewhere else though, doesn't it?" my father said. "Besides, don't worry about it. Next spring, I'll plant some grass and it'll look like a hill."

"Can grass grow on concrete?" I asked.

My father grinned and tongued at his mustache. His eyes focused on the pile again. "Well, then we'll just get some more dirt to put on it," he said. "And then we'll plant some grass." He looked down at me and smiled, as if for added effect. "And then before you know it, we'll have this yard looking just like a baseball field."

"That'd be a weird-looking baseball field," my mother said. She shook her head and glanced at my father.

He smiled and walked toward her. "What'd I tell you?" He gently put his hands on her shoulders and leaned forward until their foreheads touched. "Don't worry. I'll take care of all this. Trust me."

She rolled her eyes. "How many times have I heard that one before?"

It seemed that my dad came up with a new plan or hobby every couple of months. I was told that before I was born, he nearly became a professional forest firefighter in Wyoming. He ran several miles a day and timed himself with a stop watch in preparation for the difficult physical test fire jumpers must pass. In the end, he settled for the Pennsylvania State Forest Firefighter Certification instead, deciding that he didn't want to leave McVeytown. A few years later, he decided to try breeding rabbits. He bought a dozen rabbits, cages for them, and food. Within a few months, he sold all of them for a loss. After that, he turned his attention to goats, thinking the animals would graze on the weeds and brush that grew around Lucky's ruins. The first goat bayed and cried at all hours of the day, quieting only during her daily feeding time. The second, a massive and angry animal, broke free of its chain in our yard and escaped onto the road one night, nearly causing a car accident. And then, for a while, my father loved model rockets and spent several months painstakingly building one. On its inaugural launch, the rocket flew high into the sky, but the tiny parachute failed to deploy. It crashed into the ground and shattered.

He struggled with more than just sustaining interest in projects. He promised to do things but then came up with excuses to never even start them. He still pledged to build me a tree house—he even had easy access to wood scraps at Overhead Door. When I asked him about a tree house, he always said "some day soon" or "just wait until next summer." I begged him to teach me how to ride a bicycle—"just wait until you're a little older." If I wanted to have a water-gun battle or play catch, there was always a reason he couldn't: he had to mow the lawn, work on his truck, type an accident report, or go to the firehouse. Usually, though, it was the last excuse—the firehouse still came first.

I wondered how much time my dad would even put into the new house. I'm sure my mother worried about this as well. Though my dad talked about the project with pride, I didn't feel as excited. I was just happy that Lucky had removed his pigeons. And with the hole gone, maybe he wouldn't return to light any fires.

I had watched on the hot afternoon at the end of August when Lucky came to get his pigeons. He backed his pickup next to those firebombed walls where he housed the birds. He climbed out of his truck and then loaded large metal cages full of fluttering and gabbling birds onto the bed.

I peered out through the window, just as I had when he lit those Saturday morning fires. Like then, he wore his green painter's uniform and stuck a toothpick in his mouth—he reminded me of a cartoon character, always dressing the same. When he took a break, he sat on the tailgate and wiped his bald, sweaty head with a white hankie. That night, I asked my father what happened to the pigeons.

"Your grandfather took them to Ricky Trutt's farm," he said. "He's keeping them in a barn there."

"It took long enough," my mother said. "I wanted those stupid birds out of here for years."

My father inhaled, puffing his chest as though preparing for a fight. "Teena, it's his land. What do you want me to do?"

"More than you have been," she said.

Commercials for back-to-school sales aired on television. Two months earlier at Hershey Park, the end of summer had seemed unimaginable. Now, each day chugged by, fueled by the dread of another school year. My afternoons of watching *CHiPs*, riding the swing, and listening to my Walkman would be replaced with spelling tests and multiplication tables.

On Labor Day weekend, a friend of my father's spent the entire afternoon helping him rebuild the engine to our old lawn mower. They worked under the shade of the trees in our backyard. I walked toward them, eager to be part of their world.

Though Brad Boyer was the same age as my father, his hair had already whitened. His deep blue eyes focused on part of the engine. He looked toward me.

"Are you going to help us out?"

"Can I?" I asked.

"Just stay back," my dad said. He held up his hand, ordering me to stop. "We have parts on the ground here. I know exactly where everything is. I don't want you messing it up."

"I won't mess it up," I said.

"Take a seat," Brad said. He patted the ground. "We're taking this engine apart. Watch and learn."

For a couple of hours I sat silently while my father turned wrenches and disassembled metal parts. In the late afternoon, the sky darkened and a breeze hissed through the trees. Thunder rumbled in the distance.

"Better get inside," my dad said. "Storm's coming."

"What about the mower?" I asked.

"Brad and I will cover it with a tarp," he said. My dad looked to the sky and then back at me. "Do you know where the tarp is?"

"Yeah, in the shed, by the ladder, right?"

My dad nodded. "Do me a favor and go get it for me. Brad and I are going to get some bricks to lay down. Okay?"

I turned and ran toward the shed. Tree branches swayed in the wind. The leaves rustled. As my legs pumped, I pretended that I was just like Brad and my father. In my imagination, the shed was on fire. I burst through the door, scanned the inside, and found the blue tarp. Only it wasn't a tarp, it was a person that I had to save. I grabbed it, hugged it tight, and then ran back outside and toward my father. When the rain droplets pelted my arms, they were ash and sparks from the building—it had blown up right after I saved the person inside.

I watched as my father covered the mower and its scattered pieces. Brad placed the bricks on the edges of the tarp, making sure the wind wouldn't whip it up and send it sailing across the yard. The three of us ran into the shed, stepping inside just as the rain began to pour. Lightning cracked above the fields. We waited in silence for a few minutes.

"Hey Jay," Brad said. "Thanks for helping out. I don't think your dad and I could have done it without you." He patted my shoulder and smiled.

"I didn't do that much," I said. "Just my job." That's what my father would have said.

"Well, you'd better get paid then," Brad said. He reached into his back pocket and pulled out his wallet. He glanced at my father and smiled. "Does he have a savings account?"

"Teena and I started one for him when he was born," my dad said.

Brad pulled a twenty-dollar bill from his wallet. My heart thumped—I only saw that kind of money at Christmastime.

"I'm going to give this to your father," Brad said. "And he's going to put it into your savings account for you. One day, you'll use that money for college. It'll mean more to you then than it will now."

"Thanks, Brad," I said. I appreciated what he had done, though the twenty dollars would have been nice to have right then. I could have bought a new tape player to listen to my music on.

My father smiled and patted Brad's arm. "Thanks."

"Don't mention it. Anything for your boy."

My father's friends always went out of their way to say hello to me. At school, a few of the firemen visited classrooms each fall and handed out smoke alarms. They stood in front of the class, dressed in their bunker boots, and talked about fire safety.

"Make sure your family has an escape plan," one of the firemen, Burt Drusky, said. "And as you leave, make sure you feel every door. See if it's hot. What's it mean if the door is hot?"

I raised my hand.

Burt smiled and his cheeks reddened, matching his hair and beard. My father and I had just seen him at the store in McVeytown.

I waved my hand in the air, impatient.

"Okay, Jay, you might be cheating here, but what's it mean?"

"That there's a fire behind the door," I said. "If you open it, the flames could explode because of the fresh oxygen."

Some of the other kids raised their eyebrows, impressed—the fireman had not only known my name, but I had answered the question correctly. I knew that for the rest of the day my classmates would ask me about this. Times like that made me the most popular kid in school. No one ever picked on me. I wondered if that was because everyone knew who my father was.

On the bus rides to school, I pretended that I was the fire chief while my friend Michael was an EMT. We talked into our fists as though they were radios. I drove the fire truck over roads that had been washed out by floods, maneuvered around cattle that wandered into our path, and passed cars on the highway. At the end, whenever Michael had to get off the bus, we always managed to put out our imaginary fire or rescue someone trapped in a crashed car.

Once, after lunch, my class watched a convoy of screaming fire trucks and ambulances speed past the school. Everyone ran to the window to marvel at the scene—maybe we could see smoke.

"What's going on?" a friend asked me.

"I don't know," I said. "Must not be too bad. They only dispatched one company. I'll ask my dad tonight. He'll know."

If something happened in Mifflin County, my dad always found out about it. That meant I could tell my friends and even teachers about what happened at car accidents or how a fire started. I could let them believe that my father and I were just like any other father and son—we talked, we spent time together, he took me fishing. I don't think my father had been aware of how I parroted everything he told me. However, he found out once after I repeated something I shouldn't have.

In first grade, another classmate's uncle drove into the back of a garbage truck while drunk. I heard my father talking about the accident on the telephone.

"One of the worst I've seen," my father said. "He hit so hard that when we finally pulled him out, we saw that it'd knocked his shoes off. Killed him lickity-split."

And this is what I told my classmate during recess. That evening his mother called my house. Afterward, my parents sat me down in the kitchen and asked if I had said those things. I explained that I heard my father say all of this, that I didn't realize it was such a big deal.

"You can't just tell someone that," my mother said. "That was his uncle who died. They're very upset right now."

My father had been quiet during most of the talk. His deep green eyes focused on me. "Don't ever tell people what you hear in this house," he finally said. He then stood and left the room. But I still reported what I'd heard. If someone had been killed, I just made sure that any of the friends I told weren't related to the dead.

"Your dad sounds so cool," my friends at school would say. "It must be so exciting to have a dad that's the fire chief."

"Oh yeah," I said. I tried to adopt a voice of confidence, as if I knew all about car accidents and fires, which my friends thought sounded exciting. In fact, my dad seemed a fleeting image of the seemingly ideal fathers my friends talked about. But that was something I never told anyone.

One summer we drove past the home of one of my friends from school. He was playing catch with his father in the front yard.

"There's Ben Oswald," I said. "We should get gloves like Ben and his dad have. We could play catch sometimes." Once or twice a year my dad and I played Wiffle ball together, a thrill in itself, but I wanted the real thing—leather glove, hardball, wooden bat.

"That sounds like fun," he said. "We should do that." He never spoke of it again.

The next summer, he bought himself a new Rawlings glove for the fire company's twilight softball team. On Sundays, he left for an afternoon of practice and then a game against one of the other fire departments from Mifflin County. After their first game, he returned home sore and smiling, telling us how he had hit a double down the first-base line.

"You could practice with me in the evenings," I told him. "We could play catch or I could hit balls to you."

"We could," he said. "But you know, I'm usually pretty tired after work, kiddo."

"But you're not too tired to go to the firehouse."

He laughed, as if what I just said was ridiculous. "I have to stop at the firehouse. It's my job."

Ten

As my school bus crowned the hill before our house one afternoon, plumes of white smoke lifted into the crisp mid-September sky. My heart thumped in fear—Lucky is back, I thought, burning more mattresses or trash. But then I saw fire trucks parked on our neighbor's lawn, their strobe lights rolling. Flames tongued through a hole in the roof and licked the tops of window frames. When the school bus hissed to a stop, I ran across the road and toward our trailer. My mother waited on the tiny front porch.

"What happened?" I asked. "Is Dad there?"

"Not yet," my mother said. "The fire company just got there a few minutes ago. I bet your dad left work early to come to this."

We walked across the small field of alfalfa separating our trailer from Bill and Megan Grassmeyer's house. Firemen sprayed water on the upstairs corner of the house where flames had burned just a few minutes before. A small crowd of neighbors, including Alma Peicht, stood about twenty yards from the house and watched.

"Teena, can you believe this?" Alma asked. "I looked out the window and saw the smoke."

"Thank goodness nobody was home," my mother said.

McVeytown's tanker and engine truck idled in the driveway. An ambulance with two EMTs sat in the yard next to the trucks. Firemen rushed past us carrying a ladder, running faster than any of the ones I had watched on television. Tires squealed behind us and it seemed the whole crowd turned in unison. My dad jumped out of his pickup, leaving the door wide open. He yanked his spare turn-out coat from the box on the bed of his truck.

"There's Dad," I said. "He'll get this under control." Under control—that's how I had heard him talk about fires to his friends.

He already wore the spare set of bunker pants and boots. He threaded his arms through the red suspenders on his pants, shrugged on the heavy black coat, and then tucked his white helmet under his arm. As he walked toward the tanker truck, he snagged the coat's hooks through the D rings across his chest and then patted down the overlapping Velcro. While he talked with two other firemen, another vehicle screeched to a halt.

"Megan's father is here," Alma said. "Must have heard about it."

Rich Baumgardner owned Rich's Cars, a used-car dealership a half mile outside of McVeytown. Throughout the year, the same dozen or so trucks and sedans sat in his lot, their windows painted with prices everyone knew were too expensive. Rich ran from his car, his short legs pumping hard.

"Are they in there?" he yelled. He scratched at his short white hair and pointed at the house. "Are those kids in there?"

"Nobody was home," Alma said.

Another fireman helped my dad shrug on a heavy air tank. He had explained to me how it worked, and I loved that the acronym for self-contained breathing apparatus was SCBA, or scuba, just like the divers in the ocean. He buckled a strap for the unit around his waist and walked toward the house. The mask dangled over his chest.

Rich unbuttoned his polo shirt and breathed as though he were about to hyperventilate. He looked up at the burning roof and walked toward the house. Someone in the crowd asked what he thought that he was doing.

"There's Christmas presents up there," Rich said. His face looked red and the veins on his forehead bulged. He pointed at the house again. "Bill and Megan bought them kids Christmas presents already." He turned and almost walked into my father.

My dad pressed an open hand against Rich's chest. "Where are the presents?"

"Upstairs," Rich said. "The big bedroom. Just get out of my way, I'll get them."

"You go in there and you'll be arrested," my dad said.

"It's my daughter's house, Denton," Rich screamed. He stood

on his toes and leaned into my father's face. "I want those kids' presents and they can't arrest me for that."

"Interfering with an emergency call, keeping us from doing our job, putting yourself and maybe firemen at risk." My dad cocked his head and leaned forward. "You better believe you can get arrested for that."

My father pulled a hood from a pocket on his jacket and cloaked his head. He slid the air mask over his face. He then capped his head with his white helmet and buckled the chin-strap. He pointed at Rich and said, "Stay here."

My dad turned and jogged toward the burning home. He disappeared through the smoke that rolled out the front door, toward the pops and cracks of flames from inside. The crowd hushed. More sirens wailed in the distance, probably on their way from other fire companies in Mount Union or Strodes Mills.

I looked up at my mother; she held a hand over her mouth, eyes closed, praying. My heart felt like it rattled against my ribs and then slid down into my stomach. For me, it wasn't fear but pride—I'd never seen my father in action. A few minutes later, his white helmet emerged through the blackness as he ran with his head down as though rushing for a touchdown. Instead of a football, he cradled boxes covered in shiny, festive wrapping paper. The small crowd applauded. Alma patted my shoulder.

"That's just like your dad," she said. "Always putting others first."

Alma smiled down at me—she had meant it as a compliment to my father's devotion to helping the town. But my mother thought that this was exactly my dad's problem.

He didn't come home until well after dark that night. I lay awake in bed, listening for his rumbling engine, the screeching brakes, the slam of his truck door, and then his stomping boots on the porch steps. He stepped into the hallway, softly latched the door, and crept past my closed bedroom door.

"Where were you?" my mother asked. She sounded panicked, speaking quickly, but the words came out with force. The walls of the trailer were thin and made of heavy-duty cardboard. When they fought, I usually heard everything. "It's past eleven."

"Well, we were up at Bill and Megan's for a while," he said. I heard him ease onto one of the small, vinyl-covered chairs at the kitchen table. "I went to the station to clean up. Had to type up the report too. Figured I'd just do it there. Looks like Megan left the stove on by accident. 'Course we won't know for sure until the fire marshal looks at it tomorrow."

No one said anything for a few moments. I imagined that my mother stood against the kitchen counter, her arms folded over her chest, staring at my father. He probably fingered through the mail on the table.

"Jay in bed?" he asked. "I'm starving. What'd you guys eat? Save me anything?" He sounded as if this were just like any other night.

"What kind of example do you think you set for your son today?" my mother asked.

"What do you mean?"

"You pull in to that fire like some idiot," she said. Though the walls muffled the sound, I heard the anger in her voice. "Squealing your tires, jumping out of your truck."

"Well, I hate to tell you, but that's what you do at a fire," he said flatly. "And it was Bill and Megan. Did you expect me to just mosey on over to the fire truck?"

"No one was home," she said. "You knew that. The other firemen must've told you that. But you just had to put on a show."

"A show?" His voice rose. He probably sat at the table, staring at the tablecloth like the night he told us about the double-wide trailer.

"You put on a show for the crowd," she continued. "You wanted to look good."

I heard a thump—his hand slamming the table. "I didn't want Rich Baumgardner running in there, if that's what you mean. You know, we had to take him to the hospital after you and Jay left. He couldn't breathe. He thought he was having a heart attack. He was really sick."

"It's no wonder," she said. "You both acted like a bunch of nuts. You ran into a house to rescue presents?"

"To help our neighbors. Wouldn't you want them to do that for us?"

"If we were trapped and burning alive, I hope they'd save us. But do you honestly think that they would? Half the time Megan doesn't even look at me when I drive past. And when she does talk to me, it's to remind me how much better they have it."

"Well, our house didn't burn today," my father said. "I'd say we have it better right now. Besides, do unto others as you wish for them to do unto you, right? That means something around here. They still have at least part of a house rather than nothing at all."

After a few moments of silence, my mother softly said, "Denton, you ran into a house to save Christmas presents. Not people. Gifts."

"And those kids will have some presents at Christmas now," he said. "Do you know what it's like to lose all your toys when you're a kid? I wouldn't wish it on anybody."

"All you think about is other people."

"What about the new house? I did that for us, for you and Jay."

"And you're going to drive us into the hole to do it," she said. "We're going to be paying off the bank loan for years. I didn't even want it."

"What'd I tell you?" The chair creaked when he stood. "We're getting that house. That's all there is to it." He walked past my door and to the bathroom for a shower. Neither of them spoke the rest of the night.

It hadn't always been like this. When either of them told me stories of when they first met and began dating, I sensed that my mother's resistance to the fire company had not been there initially but had grown over the years. He told her on their first date that he was a fireman and she had assumed that it was a hobby, not a love she would have to compete against.

When they met, after high school, my dad worked at a milk-bottling plant. He lived in an apartment in Lewistown with his parents then, but made the twenty-minute drive to McVeytown at least once a day to visit the firehouse. One of the dispatchers at the firehouse told my father about a young woman named

Teena Mattern who lived outside of McVeytown. Her mother cared for a few elderly folks — no one too old or sick, just people who wanted home-cooked meals and freshly washed clothes. My dad showed up at the Mattern's house one Saturday afternoon in his old blue Buick. He knew the area well — Little Brick Road: my father had grown up in a house just one hundred yards away. And my dad immediately recognized the Mattern's home — Lucky had built it in the mid-1960s.

My father knocked on the door that day and presented my grandmother with window decals.

"Just passing through here and I heard that you took care of a few older folks," he said. "Figured I'd drop off these stickers. They're fluorescent orange. If you place them on the outside of bedroom windows, I can direct firefighters to search for occupants."

My grandmother invited him inside for some sweet tea and that's when he first saw my mother. She was young, just a few years out of high school, and working at a factory assembling airplane parts. Brown hair fell past her narrow shoulders.

"I never forgot her hair that day," he told me once. "Or her smile. The three of us talked for a while, then your mother walked me outside to my car. That's when I asked her out on a date."

"What'd you say to her?" I asked.

"Well, I just asked her. Nothing fancy about it. 'Course I was nervous she'd say no."

My parents went on their first date in September of 1978 — a meal at the firehouse. Since the company was made up of volunteers, the women's auxiliary—firemen's wives, girlfriends, sisters, and mothers—often cooked dinners and sold tickets to the public. The chicken and waffles brunch, buffet breakfasts, and holiday roasts raised money for equipment at the firehouse.

"It was a little strange for a first date," my mother once said. "But when I got to know your father, I couldn't think of anywhere else he'd have taken me."

She said my dad was funny and handsome. A few boys had taken her out on dates during high school, but my father was the first man she had ever loved. They continued dating, and by February, they were engaged. That spring, they eloped to Winchester, Virginia, and were married by the justice of the peace. After returning home, they moved into the trailer together. A few days later, my dad drove to Harrisburg—the city still in a panic after the accident at the Three Mile Island nuclear plant—and bought a Dalmatian puppy. He always joked that it was their first child.

Ford New Holland hired my dad that summer and he quit his job at the milk plant. He worked third shift and slept in the afternoon and evenings. But if a fire call beeped over his pager, he'd crawl from their bed, dress in his turn-out gear, and speed away. Though his work shift began at 11 p.m., he often showed up late and reeked of smoke and sweat. When layoffs hit the plant a few years after I was born, my mother suspected that his unreliability factored into why he was among those cut.

My mother soon realized the fire company was no mere hobby for my father—hobbies don't cost men their jobs. My dad, perhaps reading her feelings, tried to get her involved with the company. He told her that the ladies' auxiliary at the firehouse always needed help with brownie sales, meals, and fund-raisers. All the other guys' wives helped out—surely she could as well.

"When I didn't do it," my mother said, "the women thought that I was snob, that I thought I was too good for them."

Thus began a silent feud between my mother and the wives of the other firemen. In the rare instance when my mother and one of those women talked, neither seemed particularly friendly. Instead, they just exchanged hollow pleasantries about the weather or shopping.

But my mother preferred to ignore the women. Each week, we encountered at least a half-dozen people we pretended not to see; if we disregarded them at the gas station or post office in McVeytown, they would do the same for us.

"There's Sally Kenmore," my mother said. "Don't look."

And it seemed that while my dad didn't ignore my mother, he was at least emotionally vacant. For as long as I could remember, it felt as if my mother always missed my father. On the nights when my dad worked at the firehouse, she washed dishes or cleaned the house. She helped me with homework or sat next to me on the couch while we watched television. Sometimes it seemed that my parents lived in the same house but never together.

And he neglected me. When I was sick with a fever, he never held a cold washcloth on my forehead like my mother did. Once, when I had tonsillitis before the end of first grade, he spent most of the day at the firehouse. He had arranged for Life Lion helicopter, Central Pennsylvania's first emergency medical chopper, to land at the McVeytown baseball field so the community could see "just what their tax dollars paid for." He had talked about the helicopter visit for months.

I vomited every fifteen minutes that Saturday morning, gagged and coughed, and then finally felt the dizziness of dehydration. My mother crouched beside the couch and pressed a palm against my forehead.

"I'm going to have to call your father," she said. "You need to see a doctor."

She talked to him for a long time, coaxing him to leave. "He needs to see a doctor," my mother said. "I'm worried he might be dehydrated. He keeps throwing up mucus." After a few minutes, she would speak again. "Denton, I think we should both take him. We don't know how long it'll take at the emergency room." As I listened to my mother plead with my father to return home, I felt ashamed—I had ruined the day for him.

When he walked in the living room, he stared at me for a few moments. His eyes looked hard, as if he were concentrating on something.

"You're okay, aren't you squirt?"

"He's not okay," my mother said. "Let's go."

My dad drove us to the emergency room and said little. He cradled me in his arms and carried me into the hospital. After a saline drip poked my vein, my fever eased and I fell asleep. When I woke up on the couch back at home, covered with a blanket, my father was kneeling next to me, his strong hand on my shoulder.

"Hey kiddo, the helicopter's already here," he said. "I drove up to see how you're feeling."

"My throat still hurts."

"I brought some Popsicles home for you," he said. "Think you still feel like seeing the chopper?"

I nodded yes. He grinned and winked. "I thought so."

He cradled me in his arms again and carried me to his truck. I lay on the seat, my head resting on his lap, as he drove to the playground. He lifted me out of the truck and then walked me toward the blue and white helicopter. My father explained to me how joysticks and gimbals worked, though the specifics quickly faded from memory. He gently lowered me so that I could see inside the helicopter's cabin. He pointed out suction masks, fluid boxes, defibrillators, and the drug cupboard.

"This helicopter can fly to Hershey in just fifteen minutes," he said. "You remember, it takes us two hours to drive there when we go to Hershey Park."

Then he showed me the cockpit, with its LCD panels and gauges spread across what looked like a dashboard.

After I recovered from the tonsillitis, my doctor said that in order to avoid more illness, I should have my tonsils removed. And so, on the day after first grade ended, my mother drove me to the hospital for surgery. When I woke in my hospital room, I saw my mother seated in a chair by my bed.

"Where's Dad?" I asked. My throat felt as if I had swallowed sandpaper.

"He's working on his truck," she said. She explained that one of his mechanic friends offered to help my father install a rebuilt engine in my father's rundown pickup.

My mother slept on a cot next to my bed that night. Each time I woke, she sat up and asked if I was okay. I wondered where my father was, if he had come to visit and I had somehow slept through it. When I went home the next day, our driveway was empty—he hadn't returned yet. My mother helped me walk up the porch steps. She brought me water and Popsicles to ease the dry burn in my throat.

When my dad finally drove home late that afternoon, he told my mother that he had worked straight through the night and said the truck drove like new. He then walked into the living room and looked down at me on the couch.

"Dad," I said. I tried to sit up on the couch so that I could look strong.

"How are you feeling, kiddo?"

"Sick."

He nodded and inserted a video into the VCR.

"I figured you would be," he said. "I rented you this Pee Wee Herman video to watch."

"Do you want to watch it with me?"

He shook his head. "I would if I weren't so tired. I have to get into bed."

Eleven

In the evenings when my father led meetings at the fire-house, my mother and I sometimes walked to her parents' house a quarter mile away. Our trailer felt like a tiny shed compared to their house. When I was younger, I sometimes tried to tap dance on the cement floor in their basement, telling my mother that I wanted to be like Fred Astaire, whom I had watched on afternoon movies. Or else I clambered up the carpeted steps to the second floor, pretending to be a rock climber.

But most of all, I loved their yard, with the row of tall pines lining the alfalfa field on one side. A flower garden flanked their small paved driveway. It seemed as though my grandmother had planted every type of flower — daffodils, azaleas, roses, mums. The scene looked like one of the pictures on the boxes of Kodak film my mother bought: the purples and reds of the flowers and the bluish tint of the pines. No piles of concrete or old bits of foundation covered in ash like our yard, just green grass and brilliant flowers.

One night, my mother and I walked on the stones and cinders covering the berm of the road. As we neared their house, I watched my grandmother carefully walk among her flower beds and glide a sprinkling can above them, slowly going back and forth as though ironing. Her flowers always smelled like the air after a summer storm, fresh and sweet.

When I first learned to speak, I called her Nena (*knee-naw*), a name that had stuck ever since. Before retiring, she had worked in the bakery at the Giant Food Store in Lewistown, the same grocery store my mother shopped in every Friday night. She looked much younger than someone in her late fifties: tall and fit, with curled gray hair.

The three of us walked across the yard, past neatly trimmed bushes and dwarf pines. The evening crows squawked and fluttered in the trees. We stepped onto a wooden deck and entered the screened-in back porch. My grandfather sat on a chaise lounge in the corner and read the evening newspaper. His belly bulged against a white undershirt and drooped over the belt line of his jeans.

"There's my boy," he said. He removed his reading glasses, folded the newspaper, and combed his fingers through his thinning gray hair. He smelled like Old Spice aftershave and Irish Spring soap. Each evening, after he returned home from his job in the mail room at Huntingdon State Prison, he showered, then read the newspaper and watched television before bed. I called him Pap.

"How's school?" he asked. For the past few weeks, he had asked me this question every time I saw him. It became a game for us: each time he asked, I tried to invent new ways to explain just how much I hated second grade.

"Would you stop reminding him about school?" Nena said.

"What?" He smiled. Before he continued, I knew the next words out of his mouth. They had become his mantra, what he told me throughout the summer and every time I complained about school: "They're the best days of your life."

"Best part about school is summer vacation," I said.

The four of us sat quiet for a moment. Tractor trailers hummed and rattled over the highway.

"Denton at the firehouse?" Nena asked.

"Work detail," my mother said. "They're cleaning chimneys."

"You guys will have to worry about that pretty soon," Pap said. "Denton's still putting a woodstove in the basement, isn't he?"

"As far as I know," my mother said. "At least it'll be warmer than that oil furnace we have now."

"Has Denton been feeling better?" my grandmother asked, her tone softer.

"He says he is," my mother said. "He'd never tell me anyway."

"What's wrong with Dad?" I asked.

My mother glanced at Nena and then looked down at the floor. Neither of them answered and I knew that this had been something I wasn't supposed to hear.

"What's wrong with him?" I asked.

"Your dad says that his stomach has been upset lately," my mother said.

"But he's okay, right?" I asked.

"You know your dad," Pap said. "Nothing can keep him down."

My dad rarely got sick. It seemed that he never had a cold or a cough. And he had seemed fine since that day at Hershey Park four months earlier. I decided that Pap was probably right.

We talked for a bit after that, probably about the Pittsburgh Pirates or the neighbor's farm. When the sun dipped below the ridgeline, my mother stood and said that we should leave before the light disappeared.

As we walked home that night, I pointed to a silver can that glinted in the remaining light. My mother stepped into some weeds to retrieve it. She carried a balled-up plastic bag inside one of the pockets in her jeans. When we saw a soda or beer can along the side of the road, my mother placed it in the bag and then saved it for recycling. A garbage bag full of crushed aluminum cans brought around twenty dollars.

"We should save the money we get from these cans," I said. "Then I could get a new bike."

She upended a half-full Coors Light can and poured the beer onto the ground. It smelled like the rotten apples that fell from the trees in our yard. She shook out the last drops, pulled out the bag from her pocket, and placed the can inside. "Your dad always says that he'll show you how to ride one some day."

"Yeah," I said. "He always tells me that."

• • •

Much of what my dad knew about carpentry, wiring, or plumbing he had learned from working with Lucky. My father had built a shed for the riding lawn mower several years earlier. The plywood structure, capped with a sheet metal roof, looked as though a strong wind could blow it over, but somehow it had remained intact. For the past several months, my father spent a few hours each week at the kitchen table drawing crude blueprints for the wires and pipes he planned to install in the new double-wide.

By mid-October the backhoes had not only excavated the hole but had also dug large trenches where drainage pipes would be laid. Bundles of white pipes and pallets of cinder blocks sat in the dirt next to the hole. My dad had found a husband-and-wife team of bricklayers, both of whom looked close to retirement, to build the foundation of the new house. They had already poured the cement floor, which looked smooth and flat, just like Pap and Nena's basement. The pair now worked at laying the walls. In the evenings, after my father came home, we walked around the hole and inspected their progress, which usually looked minimal.

"How long's it take to do this?" I asked.

"Shouldn't be more than a few weeks," my dad said. "If the weather's good."

"It barely looks like they're doing anything."

"Well, it's slow, especially with only two people."

"Can't you get more people?" I asked.

"This is expensive work and these were the cheapest people I could find," he said. "You know, I'm trying to do a lot of this myself so that I don't have to pay even more."

When we finished looking into the hole, I followed him back

to the trailer. The leaves on the oak trees had turned orange and yellow. With each gust of wind, walnuts thumped to the ground in the front yard, apples in the back.

"Want to ride to Harshbarger's with me?" my dad asked.

Harshbarger's Hardware Store sat next to the firehouse. It was small, maybe twice the size of our trailer, but as my dad always said, it had the best selection of building supplies in McVeytown. Of course, it also was the only hardware store in town. I followed my father through the cramped aisles. He filled small paper bags with handfuls of nails and grabbed a special crayon he told me was used for marking cinder blocks and cement.

"You ready, squirt? Let's head home. Your mother probably has dinner about ready for us."

When I turned to walk toward the cash register, I saw Lucky standing at the end of the aisle, his hands dug inside his pockets, as if he had been watching us.

My father stiffened and glanced toward the floor. "Dad, what are you doing here?"

"Your mother and I came up for supper at the Country Kitchen," Lucky said. Country Kitchen, a tiny restaurant, sat just outside McVeytown along Route 522. Each time we passed the place, the smell of grease seemed to permeate my dad's truck.

"Where's Mom at?" my dad asked.

"Pissing," Lucky said. "She drinks coffee like it's going out of style. I just stopped in here to grab a few things quick. How's the new place?"

"Coming right along," my dad said. "Hopefully they'll get most of the foundation laid before the snow comes."

"Need any help with it? I can come up in the evenings. I'd even charge you less than my standard rate."

My father blinked and cleared his throat. "I think we'll handle it all right. I'm about to put down pipe for the septic tank. Aren't there two tanks?"

"The old house had two," Lucky said. "Should be about ten yards from the road. They're not far apart. I'll come up and help you look for them."

"You don't have to drive up just for that."

"How would you ever find them?" Lucky snapped. "I'll come up. But what are you doing that for now anyway? You're not moving in until next year."

"Yeah, but I want to get it done before the ground freezes."

Lucky looked toward the front of the store. "Woman," he yelled. "Hey. Come here."

Helen squeezed through the narrow aisle, her hips rubbing against hammers and tape measures. She smiled as though she hadn't seen us in years. "Denton and Jay, oh what a surprise. What are you doing here? We just ate at Country Kitchen."

"Just getting some stuff for the new house," my father said.

Helen opened her mouth to speak but burped instead. "Pardon me," she said. "I had to rift." She swallowed and then continued. "Working on the new house, that's wonderful. Is the fire company getting ready for the fair?" The third week of October always marked the beginning of the Rothrock Fair in McVeytown, which was sponsored by the fire company.

"We've got a chicken and waffle dinner one night," my father said. "It's Friday. Maybe you and Dad will want to come to that."

"Just think, Halloween will be here soon," Helen said and smiled. "Are you ready for Halloween, Jay? Have a costume picked out? Lucky, remember last year he was a clown? Denton brought him down to the hotel. Wasn't that special?"

"When he came in," Lucky said, pointing at me, "I didn't even know he had a costume on. Looked the same as he always does."

"How's second grade?" Helen asked.

"It's good," I said. "There's a lot—"

Lucky rolled his eyes and interrupted me. "Your mother and I have some big news for you."

"We bought a house this week," Helen said, her smile big. "And guess where it is?"

"McVeytown," Lucky said. "Gonna sell the hotel and retire. Figure we might as well return home. McVeytown always was home."

I could feel my stomach tense. Not McVeytown, I thought. Not here.

"No kidding," my dad said. He scratched at his neck and nodded. "Wow. Back to McVeytown. That's great. Which house is it?"

"It's that one right next to Country Kitchen," Lucky said. "As much as your mother likes to eat there, we can save some money on gas."

"Just think how much more often we'll see each other," Helen said. She turned to me and leaned forward a bit, as much as her fat stomach would allow. "Don't you want to see your grandma more?"

"Sure," I said.

"Speak up, boy," Lucky said. "You always sound like you're scared to talk around me. You got to speak up if you ever want someone to pay attention to you."

They would live just over a mile away, much closer than their apartment in Lewistown. Those trips to the hotel would stop, which made me happy, but they would be living right down the road from us. Lucky might show up at any moment, hauling trash and a can of gasoline. Maybe he'd even bring Ricky Trutt with him. I wouldn't be allowed outside to play — my mother would make me stay inside with the doors locked. Helen would beg us to stop by and see them. She would grill me with questions, prying into my life at school and my friendships. And she would kneel in front of me, smiling, and ask for a hug. I felt suddenly that life was about to get much harder.

On the drive home, my father sang along to Jim Croce on the radio and tapped along with the beat on the steering wheel. When he told my mother about his parents' new house in McVeytown, she stared at the kitchen table, silent.

"Looks like we'll be seeing more of them," my father said. He seemed pleased about the idea. "Boy, I never thought they'd move back to McVeytown."

"No," my mother said softly. "Not in a million years."

Twelve

Many nights, when my father told my mother and me that he needed to "hop into town quick" for gas or milk, he didn't return home for an hour. It wasn't just the conversations with friends that slowed him down; he liked to drive around and "just make sure everything's okay." My mother called those trips "patrols," and I thought again of *CHiPs*, how the motorcycle cops drove the Los Angeles freeways. They were in search of law breakers. My father sought fire.

"Can I go with you?" I would ask him.

"Oh, I shouldn't be long," he said. "Just a quick little trip."

It would be a great story to tell my friends at school — I rode into town with my dad last night, just looking for a fire. Each October, he took me to the town fair with him, something that made me feel just as important as that day we rode together in the parade.

Though held in October, the Rothrock Fair always seemed the crowning end to summer as well as the end of any hope of warm weather again until March. The Ferris wheel, the sole ride at the fair, sat on home plate at the McVeytown playground. When the wheel's operator took our tickets, we walked up the metal ramp and then after we sat down he locked a metal bar across our laps. The engine whirred to life, seemingly churning my father and me into the sky. Below us, the scene expanded like a miniature version of Hershey Park. Instead of bright neon, the fair looked washed in a dirty yellow glow. As we rose still higher, a chilly breeze cut through the night.

Food booths clustered along the third-base line of the Little League infield, selling hot sausage sandwiches, cotton candy, and funnel cakes. A few yards away near the visitors' dugout, teenagers and rough-looking men lined up for a dollar sledge-hammer swing at the hood of a wrecked car. Midway games lined the outfield fence: Skee-Ball, a ring toss, a dart game with balloons. Far off, near the grass parking lot in the Junior Babe Ruth outfield, the fire company ran a dunking booth. My father had already spent five dollars trying to knock Art Kenmore into the water.

Just as we were about at the peak of the Ferris wheel, we jerked to a stop, causing our seat to sway. I grasped the lap bar until my knuckles turned white.

"You scared?" my dad asked.

"No," I said, unable to look down. I stared ahead, past the parking lot, beyond the speeding headlights of cars on the highway, and focused on the faint hint of a blue ridgeline against an almost black sky.

"I think I've been to this fair every year," my dad said. "Must be twenty years now. And each year, they've had this same Ferris wheel, the same games."

The wheel jerked forward and we slowly descended. After a few more rotations, we stopped at the bottom and the wheel operator unlocked our lap bar.

We walked through the small crowd, toward the parking lot, until my father stopped and began to laugh. Art Kenmore tramped toward us, his shoulders hunched underneath a pink bathrobe. Wet hair was plastered to his head, and when he stood before us I heard his teeth chatter.

"What in the world is that thing?" my dad asked. "You look like a drowned Easter Bunny."

"It's a robe," Art said. "Someone finally knocked me into that stupid dunking booth. The wife went home and got me this. She said I'd catch pneumonia if I walked around wet all night."

"You might want to," my dad said. "Enough people see you in that and you'll never live it down."

"You know how wives are," Art said, rolling his eyes. "Has to stick me in this thing? I think I'd have been just fine."

My dad nodded and toed at the ground. "Sounds just like Teena. I've heard all that bellyaching before, believe me. They say that 'I am' is the shortest sentence in the English language. Know what the longest is? 'I do.'"

Art smiled and nodded. "Ain't that the truth?"

"So you helping out with the chicken and waffles tomorrow night?"

"You know it," Art said. "The auxiliary is going to start cooking in the afternoon. Hopefully we can pack them in."

"We made out pretty good last year," my dad said. "And if we want to get a new tanker, we'll have to do good tomorrow too." He paused, arched an eyebrow, and looked at Art again. "You know, maybe you can wear that robe, do a dance or something so people will throw some dollar bills at you."

"You wish." Art smiled and shook his head. "I'll see you tomorrow then, Dent. You too, Jay."

I followed my dad to the parking lot. He boosted me into the passenger side of his truck and then climbed into the driver's side, buckled his seat belt, and turned the key. The engine ground for a few seconds and then growled to life. He revved the gas.

"Buckled up?" he asked. "Want to cruise around a little? Check out the town?"

My dad made a left onto John Street and passed a dozen or so homes—ranchers, trailers, two-story houses with garages. Each yard had been decorated for fall: jack-o'-lanterns glowed on front porches; dead brown cornstalks were tied around light posts; and gourds rested in windowsills. We passed the brick Methodist church on the left, the stained-glass window unlit that night. Next door to it, the Presbyterian church sat dark as well.

When we pulled in front of Rothrock High School, my dad stopped the truck. Some of the kids at school had told me stories about their older brothers who had snuck inside Rothrock and waded through the flooded basement. He stared a moment, as if thinking back on his past, and then pressed the gas.

By the time we pulled into our driveway, it was already close to nine—my bedtime. Before sleep, I kissed my father's forehead like I did every night. He sat at the kitchen table, reading over the day's mail.

"Good night, kiddo," he said. "Be good tomorrow."

"Are you going to the fair again?"

"Yep, chicken and waffles tomorrow night, so I might not see you," he said. "You'll probably be asleep by the time I get back."

But I wasn't. The next night, he came home early; it was barely even dark yet. His face looked pale and tired as he told my mother and me what had happened. He said that while helping serve the dinner, he felt his abdomen tense with a sudden stomachache.

"It wasn't that bad at first," he said. "I thought maybe I caught a bug or something."

He said that he had felt run-down over the past few days. Planning the McVeytown Volunteer Fire Company booth for the Rothrock Fair hadn't exactly been easy for him. There had been schedules to balance with the other men, sign-up sheets for the different events—chicken and waffles on Friday and plans for barbecue chicken on Saturday. Plus the company had to wax the fire trucks for display, yet another task my father had inherited as fire chief. He even had to remind some of the guys to make sure their wives, girlfriends, or mothers ironed their uniforms and polished their shoes.

But as he stood behind the long counter of the booth "shooting the breeze" with some friends from town, the sight of the gluey waffle batter became near noxious. After he watched one of his men ladle thick gravy over sliced chicken and golden waffles, my father ran from the booth into the grass parking lot and vomited.

He shook his head and said, "I don't know what got into me."

Before bed, I kissed his forehead, and the skin felt moist and cool on my lips. I worried that he wasn't sleeping enough or eating right—those were two things my mother always made sure I did, or else I would get sick.

"You feeling better?" I asked him.

"You know me," he said, and patted my head. "Fit as a fiddle. I have to be."

A few weeks after the fair, however, the stomach pain only increased. My dad's appetite seemed to vanish—his cheeks hollowed and his eyes looked sunken. His once snug T-shirts now looked baggy. His waistline shrank and his jeans hung limply. At dusk, as he stepped out of his old pickup, his long legs seemed to move slower than usual. He winced when he eased down into his La-Z-Boy. He unlaced his boots and slid them off with a thump to the floor. Then he fell asleep with a copy of *Firehouse* magazine on his chest.

My mother shook him awake. "What's wrong? You never sleep like this."

"Just closed my eyes for a second," he said. He smiled and blinked a few times.

"You should see a doctor."

"Doctor?" He sighed and shook his head. "I don't have time to see some doctor. Besides, don't you find it a little weird that doctors call what they do 'practice'?"

"Don't joke about this," my mother said.

He tongued at his mustache and looked at my mother. "All right. When I find the time, I'll go. But I'm going to be busy this week."

One night at dinner in mid-November he shook his head and blinked his eyes to stay awake.

"Well, I can tell you one thing," he said. "I'm not missing buck season because of this."

"You're not going, are you?" my mother asked. The first Monday after Thanksgiving marked the annual start of deer-hunting season. For two or three days, my dad would stay at a cabin owned by my uncle Jed, my mother's brother. It was one of the few times each year when he was out of communication with the firehouse, and when he used his sick days from Overhead Door.

"I've gone buck hunting every year since I was twelve," my dad said. "I can't miss it."

"You never get one anyway," I said. My father hadn't shot a deer since before my birth. It'd become a running joke between us.

"Just you wait until you go out there in a couple of years," he said. He waved his fork and smiled. "Even if you do see one, you still have to be a good shot."

"But you never even see any," I said.

"Well, you just never know, this might be my year."

That week, just before his thirty-first birthday, my dad finally went to the doctor. He was anesthetized and the doctor inserted a camera down my father's throat that snaked through his insides for clues. My father brought home a videotape of the procedure and watched it on our TV.

"That's my stomach," he told me, freeze-framing the image. He crouched in front of the screen and stared at what looked like wet red walls. "Can you believe that? Bet you never thought you'd see the insides of your dad's stomach."

"Did they find anything?" I asked.

"An ulcer. They gave me some drugs, should clear it up," he said and snapped his fingers. "Just like that and I'll be all better."

My dad went buck hunting that year and, once again, returned with nothing to show for it. The ulcer medication seemed to work—his appetite returned and he quickly added back the pounds he had lost. Work on the hole in our yard stopped for the winter. The cement wouldn't form in the cold weather, my dad said. The bricklayers hoped to return in February and finish the cinder-block walls for the basement. My dad had planned on digging the septic tank and hooking up the pipes before winter. Now, he would have to wait until warmer weather.

Lucky and Helen visited on Christmas Eve.

"Ho, ho, ho," Lucky said. He stepped into the living room and removed his corduroy coat. He wore black dress pants and a white long-sleeved button-down shirt. Helen, holding plastic bags full of gifts, followed him inside and smiled. With her mouth open in surprise, she stared at the Christmas tree standing in the corner of the living room.

"Oh, Lucky, look at their tree. Isn't that special?"

"That a real one?" Lucky asked.

My dad shook his head. "Artificial one this year."

Lucky examined the tree, twisting the plastic pine needles in his fingers, and nodded. "Probably better. Those real ones burn up pretty fast. Could be a hazard."

My mother carried a chair from the kitchen table into the living room and placed it in front of the television. She sat down and crossed her arms, looking impatient.

Lucky walked past her and sank into the couch. He slipped off his polished dress shoes. Helen carefully placed the presents on the floor and then sat next to Lucky. Her weight caused his body to tilt a moment before he repositioned himself.

He turned to her. "Well, get the presents out, let's go."

Helen shifted her weight again and then stood. She furrowed her brow as if thinking about what to say next. "Denton, I'm going to use the toilet first." She walked through the kitchen and toward the bathroom.

I sat cross-legged in front of the artificial tree and wondered what they would give me this year. Like most kids, my year revolved around Christmas and whatever gifts I would receive, yet whatever Lucky and Helen had given me in the past had been so insignificant, I couldn't even recall it.

"You excited about the new house?" Lucky asked. He looked toward my mother. She stared at the window, not paying attention. "Hey woman, I asked you something."

"Teena?" my dad said. "Dad asked you something."

"Get the wax out of your ears," Lucky said. "You want this new house or not?"

My mother looked toward Lucky. "Yes. It should be nice."

The four of us sat, waiting on Helen, when we heard what sounded like a thick burst of air or a tear of paper. I looked toward my mother—she sighed and closed her eyes. My dad sat still, as if nothing had happened.

"What was that?" I asked.

"Farting," Lucky said. His voice was loud and angry. "Helen. Helen, close the door. You want the whole world to hear your bowels?"

When Helen finally returned, she pulled three boxes from her plastic bag and handed one each to my father, mother, and me. I recognized the wrapping paper—she made sure we carefully undid the tape so that she could reuse the paper each Christmas.

Lucky stood up. "Going to the car. Have to get another present."

With my grandfather gone, my parents and I opened the packages in unison and seemed to look at one another at the same time. The three of us each held a red sweatshirt. In big block white lettering, the front of my shirt read BOY.

"Lucky helped me with this," Helen said. "I think they're just darling. Go on, show each other."

My father's shirt read DAD; my mother's said MOM.

"I think it was such a cute idea," Helen said. "When you go to Hershey Park, you can each wear your shirt. Isn't that a nice idea?"

"Yeah," my dad said. "That's great, Mom."

"We can't wear a sweatshirt," I said. "Not to Hershey Park. It'll be ninety degrees when we go. We'd sweat our heads off."

Lucky walked back inside carrying a large box. I couldn't imagine what my grandparents would ever buy that might be so big. Lucky stood next to me, holding the box above my head.

The package slipped from his hands and I ducked out of the way. It crashed on the floor next to me.

He stared a second and then said, "Open it, boy." It sounded like a threat.

I opened the box. Inside was a stationary punching bag, a flimsy thing that stood four feet tall and looked too hard to actually punch. I stared at it, disappointed yet again.

"Isn't that special?" Helen said. "Lucky always does pick such nice gifts."

"I figure he needs to build coordination," Lucky said. "You're a puny boy."

My dad walked Lucky and Helen outside when they left. My mother and I looked at each other for a moment.

"If you want, I'll tape a picture of Lucky to the punching bag," she said. "Maybe that'll give you some motivation. I know I'd rather punch something with his face on it."

We were still laughing when my dad came back inside.

When February came, not only was the ground still frozen, but my father discovered that he had bought the wrong pipes for the septic tank. He also had to locate the well so that we could have running water. Lucky had promised to show him the location, but was too busy packing and readying for his own move. My dad called a friend with a backhoe to dig up the septic tanks and well—an expense he had hoped to save by doing the job himself—and ordered new pipes. He explained all of it to my mother at dinner one night.

"What can go wrong will go wrong," he said. "But don't worry. It'll be ready in time."

"Is it ever going to be finished?" I asked. "It seems like you've spent years on this."

"Sure it is," he said. "Don't worry. The new house will be here in March."

"The trailer," my mother said. "And it has to be here by March. The dealership wants it off the lot. They're bringing it no matter what."

"First off, it's going to look just like a house," he said. "Second, when it comes, I can hook a lot of the electrical stuff up myself. That'll save some money."

My dad explained that he wanted to furnish the basement. He envisioned a corner office for himself, a play area for me, a separate area for his tools. He would run phone line, cable, and install electrical outlets and lights.

"Do you even know how to do all of this?" my mother asked. Her eyes looked worried. "It'll be safe?"

"Trust me," my father said. "I'm the fire chief. Safety's my middle name. And I learned it all from Dad."

When the temperature finally began to rise, the rain turned our yard into a muddy mess. Lucky showed up one evening to help my father lay the new pipe. Like I did every time Lucky came to our house, I watched from the living room window. He drove his truck over our yard, bouncing over dips and holes, before the wheels finally sank in the mud. I watched as Lucky gunned the gas—the tires sank lower and his engine growled angrily.

"Lucky's stuck," I said.

My mother walked up behind me and sighed. "I am so sick of this mud and dirt. And this stupid house. I'm sick of it. We're not even going to be able to afford this."

My dad slowly hobbled in the mud behind Lucky's truck. It looked like the two argued with each other, though we couldn't hear anything.

"Get your coat," my mother said. "We're going to Pap and Nena's. I need to get away from here."

The faint scent of coffee always lingered in Pap and Nena's kitchen. Antiques decorated the rooms. Wooden crafts my grandparents had made—he sawed them out of wood, she painted them—decorated the walls: roosters, cows, farmhouses, Amish men, and hearts.

That night, we sat at the island in my grandparents' kitchen and talked. When my mother told them about Lucky's stuck pickup, Nena raised her eyebrows and bit her lip to hold back laughter. She stood and grabbed a coffee mug off the counter.

"Dad says he doesn't know if the septic tank will be hooked up in time," I said.

"It better be," my mother said. "This was all his idea."

"Don't worry, Teena," Pap said. "Denton knows what he's doing."

"But what'll we do about a bathroom?" I asked. "What if it's not hooked up? We might need an outhouse."

Pap laughed until his cheeks reddened. "You don't need an outhouse," he said. He flashed me a confident grim. "If Lucky's truck is out there in the yard, just go and piss in it."

My mother gasped and then laughed.

"Don't say that!" Nena snapped.

"I never did care for that man," Pap said.

"Why?" I asked.

Pap furrowed his forehead, thought a moment, and then told me the truth about Lucky.

Thirteen

Here's what I learned:

One Saturday afternoon in the mid-1960s, Lucky parked his new Studebaker in Licking Creek State Park, about a half-hour drive from McVeytown. He loved the outdoors, especially hunting—he had killed deer, turkey, rabbit, pheasant, and grouse, and in the spring and summer, he trapped muskrat, skinning their bodies and then selling the hides. He grabbed his fly rod and creel from the backseat of the car and headed toward a mountain stream. Hours later, he told the police that when he reemerged from the thick underbrush, he saw that his Studebaker had caught fire. Only the charred frame and seat springs survived.

Nobody had any cause to disbelieve Lucky. He had fought

for the army in World War II, returning home to marry his high school sweetheart, Helen. They bought two acres of land outside of McVeytown and Lucky built their home. In 1949, the couple had their first child, a daughter named Rose, who died not long after. In the years that followed, Lucky began working as a contractor. Business was good—Lucky even built a workshop about thirty yards from the house he and Helen now shared with three young sons. Everyone in McVeytown knew Lucky. They probably would have called him a good guy—he was a hard worker and a family man.

But a few months after that day in Licking Creek, a garden shed in McVeytown caught fire—it sat adjacent to a house Lucky was rebuilding. The shed mysteriously erupted in flames just after Lucky left for home one evening. Though no one else seemed to connect the stories, Lucky knew that he had gotten away with setting the fires. It must have thrilled him.

The workshop Lucky built almost doubled the size of the family's house. He stored most of his tools inside—band saws, table saws, electrical and plumbing supplies. For his first really big fire, Lucky burned this workshop to the ground. He blamed it on an electrical short—with his experience in construction, Lucky would have known how to disguise the cause. It tricked the insurance investigators—they found nothing suspicious. Throughout that winter, the pile of debris—ash, melted PVC pipe, puckered and charred wood—sat untouched, a kind of testament to Lucky's new passion.

. . .

The spring after that workshop fire, my father—only nine or ten at the time—boarded the school bus one morning along with his brothers. Helen then left for the grocery store in nearby Lewistown. But Lucky stayed at home longer than usual, not showing up at the house he was remodeling in McVeytown until close to noon. Not long after he had heaved a toolbox from the bed of his pickup truck, he heard the sirens of fire engines. Someone called a neighbor near the work site and a man yelled out the window to Lucky, "Your house is on fire."

By the time Lucky arrived home, only a brick chimney rose from the smoldering pile of rubble. Years later, this would be the spot where my father opted to place the double-wide trailer.

I imagine that Lucky, Helen, and their sons must have lived with family in the months that followed—Helen had some sisters in the area—or perhaps the family stayed at the Coleman Hotel, which they owned by that point. Lucky designed a new home for his family, one that would sit on the same two-acre stake of land; the debris from the workshop remained, as did the rubble of the first house. Throughout that fall, Lucky worked. On Saturdays, people from McVeytown parked in the yard, lugged toolboxes from their trucks, and laced work belts around their waists, ready to help their neighbor rebuild. They might have thought that Lucky simply had a string of bad luck. Or maybe they wondered if he was even a good carpenter—his buildings had a way of catching fire.

At Christmastime, Lucky and Helen held an open house for the completed home. The woodworking inside was supposedly beautiful, all of it done by hand. Lucky had built the stairs, cupboards, and banisters, seemingly sparing no expense to give his family the best home possible.

"How'd you manage to afford all this material?" someone asked Lucky.

He shrugged and said, "Insurance money."

A few years later, Lucky burned that second house.

On that day, one of their neighbors, Roy Peicht, looked out his kitchen window and saw smoke rolling from the house. When he realized that the fire had yet to fully engulf the home, he ran across two fields, hoping to help save some of the family's possessions.

Lucky stood on the front lawn under a walnut tree. His right hand jingled the change in the pocket of his painter's paints. The thumb of his left hooked a belt loop.

Roy grabbed Lucky's arm.

"Come on," Roy said. He huffed for breath and felt the heat against his skin. "We can try to save something."

"Don't," Lucky said. He stared at the house and jabbed a toothpick between his lips. "Let it burn."

Officially, the workshop and the first house fire had been ruled accidental; the fire marshal found electrical shorts. Still, people must have suspected that Lucky Varner was a firebug: the car, the shed, the workshop, the house—a lot of coincidence. It seemed everything Lucky touched turned to flames. After the second house fire, however, the police charged Lucky with insurance fraud and arson. He pleaded no contest in court and was sentenced to five years in Huntingdon State Prison, where Pap worked.

After Lucky was released, he moved into an apartment in Lewistown with Helen and my father, then a junior in high school. His brothers, Curt and Russ, had already escaped from Mifflin County. Eventually my father married my mother and moved back to that same piece of land where Lucky had burned down those three buildings.

Life seemed to go on as if nothing had ever happened. Every Sunday morning, Lucky and Helen attended church in McVeytown. Lucky went back to work, both at the hotel and as a self-employed contractor.

But that spark still burned inside him. My stomach chilled and I thought of Lucky's Saturday morning blazes. I imagined our trailer burning down and then imagined my father losing everything. When my dad reminisced about his childhood, which he did rarely, it was those younger years that my father liked to talk about—it was as if the good memories simply ended at some point. Now I understood why. My fear of Lucky boiled into a steaming hatred.

After my grandparents told me that story, we sat in silence for what felt like several minutes. I replayed all of what I had just learned, trying to somehow figure out why Lucky had lit those fires and why it had taken so long for someone to tell me the truth.

"How do you know about all of this?" I asked.

"Everyone around here knows it," Nena said. "People know about Lucky Varner."

"Plus for years I saw him every day at work," Pap said. "At the prison."

At one point, before my parents married, Pap looked up Lucky's criminal record and memorized his identification number. Pap also remembered Ricky Trutt and said that most of the prisoners hated "men like him."

"Why did they hate Ricky Trutt?" I asked. "What'd he do?"

Nena stirred her coffee and acted as though she didn't hear my question. My mother eyed the countertop. Finally, Pap sipped from his steaming mug and cleared his throat.

"Ricky Trutt's hurt little boys who were your age," my grandfather said. "He touched them in places he shouldn't have."

Nena frowned in disapproval. "I don't know how someone could ever bring a person like him around their own grandson."

I shook my head, numbed by what I had just heard, piecing together the stories. Some of it made sense — no wonder Lucky lit those fires every Saturday; he liked to burn things. And my mother locked the door when Ricky Trutt came around because she feared what he might do to me.

But I still thought of my dad — how he had saved the Grass-meyers' Christmas presents that day, and how he had said that it was awful to lose everything. My grandfather started fires, but my father put them out.

"Is this why Dad became a fireman?" I asked.

My mother nodded. "Probably. I know Helen really pushed him into it. She thought that it would make the Varners look better if your father became a fireman. If Helen tells your father to jump, he'll ask how high."

"So that's why he leaves for fires all the time," I said. "Because of her."

"Your dad's a good man," Pap said. "Don't be angry at him. Most of this isn't his fault."

"Your father means well," Nena said. "He just has his priorities mixed up. But Pap's right, your father is a very good man and he loves you."

We sat in silence again. I thought more about Lucky and those fires. It seemed strange to me that my father wanted to place our new house exactly where Lucky had burned his old one. I just couldn't understand it all.

"Why did Lucky do it?" I asked. "Why would Lucky burn down his own house?"

"He's sick," my mother said. "Your grandfather's a sick a man. He enjoys it somehow, just like you enjoy playing with Matchbox cars."

I was only seven when I learned all of this. I didn't know anything about pyromania. Years later, I would read about pyromania and understand that it was a disease of the mind. My grandfather battled it for years. I learned that little is known about the root of pyromania—some evidence suggests an early environmental factor in childhood, such as abuse or a learning disability. Other research claims that lighting fires causes euphoria that an individual might otherwise never experience

owing to poor social or sexual skills. Pyromaniacs, often believed to feel sadness and loneliness, are sometimes struck by
an intense rage that can only be quenched by starting a blaze.
They do not seek monetary gain through insurance fraud, do
not attempt revenge, and do want to cover up other crimes.
They enjoy watching the beguiling, dancing flames and give
little thought to the resulting destruction or even death.

A true pyromaniac, like my grandfather, simply loves fire.
The tension prior to striking a match arouses them. Gasoline
smells like perfume, the radiating heat feels like hot breath
against their face. A good fire blazes with uncontrollable passion, whipping palls of black smoke into the sky, swallowing
houses in minutes, a beautiful ruin that never burns the same
way twice. But a fire starter's greatest joy is the response — they
are drawn to firefighters and fire stations. A pyromaniac is grati-
fied by the orchestrated chaos of screaming fire trucks, of men
dressed in turn-out gear dashing about and dragging hoses over
their shoulders, of the people who extinguish their beautiful
living, breathing, flaming creation.

That was my grandfather. That was my father's legacy. And
now it was mine.

Fourteen

I didn't see the double-wide arrive. One afternoon at the start of March, my school bus screeched to a stop. Some of the other kids said, "Whoa" or "Look at that." The trailer sat on the foundation and looked as if someone had sawed it in half—it was split in two. Some men worked on the outside of the trailer, placing siding. My dad walked among them, wearing his tool belt.

"Knocked off early today," my dad told me.

"Can I see it?"

"Not yet," he said. "It's not safe yet. We're putting it together. But in a few days, we'll move everything in."

That next weekend, my parents worked to move most of our belongings across the yard and into the double-wide. My mother silently carried boxes—her face looked hard, as if she resented that the day had finally come. On Saturday, Pap and Nena helped us move the beds and furniture. Stepping inside for the first time, it felt as if we were leaving some part of our lives behind in favor of something greater.

"This is it," my dad said. He turned to my mother, smiling, but she walked ahead without displaying any emotion.

"It's big," I said.

"You bet it is," my dad said. "Bigger than that other junk box we lived in."

Our new living room could hold a couch and two chairs. There was a dining room—no more eating in the kitchen, like in the old trailer. Our bathroom even had a skylight. The basement was incredible—a playroom almost all my own.

A smell of newness hung in the air—the scent reminded me of opening crisp books at the beginning of each school year. And the carpet, soft and thick, sifted through my toes like sand.

Pap and Nena gave us a new couch and matching chair—none of our other furniture ever matched. Lucky and Helen gave us an old floor-model television from the hotel that looked like it weighed about a thousand pounds.

"Say good-bye to long underwear and corduroy pants," my dad said. "These windows are double-paned. The drafts won't seep in now."

We burned firewood in the woodstove in the basement and our new double-wide smelled faintly like my dad after he returned home from fires. But even with the woodstove and an oil furnace, it seemed that we could never warm the upstairs of the house. My mother endured the cold and said nothing. She wore her jacket inside the house during the day, turned up the electric blanket on their bed at night. I think she secretly felt vindicated—my dad's promises of a grand new double-wide life already seemed empty.

One morning a week after we moved in, while my dad sat on our living room couch and tied the laces on his steel-toed boots, he closed his eyes and doubled over. He gently rocked back and forth, as if trying to work the hurt out of his body.

"Dad?"

"My stomach," he said. He moaned and winced. "Smarts pretty good." He tried to force a smile.

The cramps and nausea had come back while he rushed to finish the new house. "I'll just work through it," he had said.

But now the sickness had amped up. The pain continued for hours, and then days. At first, he chalked it up to stress, assuming that the ulcer had returned—a plausible self-diagnosis, since he had worked himself raw that winter. Overhead Door showed no signs of slowing down; many weeks he worked overtime. He only declined extra work if the shift interfered with a commitment at the firehouse.

On some days, he returned home from work with a full lunch box. The sandwiches, potato chips, and Mountain Dew that my mother had packed for him all remained untouched. At dinner, he forked at his food, sipped water, and said that he just wasn't hungry. After another week, he took an afternoon off work and went to the doctor again. Maybe another ulcer, the doctor had said. He told my father that the best way to fight it was to relax. My dad didn't listen.

"Denton, you need to take care of yourself," my mom said. "You can't be running yourself into the ground."

"It'll be fine," he said. "Besides, I promised my parents that I'd help them out."

The next weekend, he moved Helen and Lucky into their new house outside McVeytown. He spent all day Saturday and Sunday hauling their furniture on his truck and then unloading it with Lucky's help. Throughout it all, the stomach pains continued; the headaches and fatigue worsened. He lost even more weight than he had the previous fall.

One afternoon, after blowing his nose, he pulled the tissue away and saw blood. He called for my mother, sat down on the floor, and titled his head against the wall. I crouched next to him, terrified. It looked like someone had punched him in the nose. Blood had already saturated the tissue, streaked down the hand that held it in place, and begun to color his wrist and shirt. He pinched his nose and sounded nasally when he talked.

"Get washcloths," he said. "And cold water. Fill a basin with cold water."

"Why cold water?" I asked.

"The cold slows the capillaries and veins," he said. "Know how your hands get so cold in the winter? That's why—your blood flow slows."

My mother knelt beside him, replaced the dripping and bloody tissue with a washcloth that she had soaked in cold water. We waited. Minutes passed, more washcloths, and the basin's water looked red. My father pinched a clean washcloth to his nostrils and closed his eyes.

"I don't get it," he said. "This should clot."

His skin began to look like clay and the hand that pinched those washcloths trembled. I wondered how long it would take for him to bleed to death.

"I don't think this is an ulcer," he said, and rolled his eyes toward my mother.

His pupils looked glassy and dilated. The strong man who had carried me to see that helicopter when I was sick suddenly looked tired, weak, and sad. An hour later, the bleeding stopped. My father slowly stood, gently washed the dried blood from his nose, mouth, and chin, and then slept on his La-Z-Boy the rest of the night.

His face looked washed in exhaustion — blue crescent pouches formed under his eyes, and the lids looked permanently heavy. He took several days off work and underwent tests at Lewistown Hospital. The doctors, concerned about my dad's low white blood-cell count, ordered a CAT scan, spinal tap, X-rays, and fed another camera into his stomach. He returned home tired and sore, moving slowly and saying he felt like a pin cushion. After all the tests, his doctors called and said that they had found nothing. Deep blue and purple bruises appeared on his arms and legs. My dad had no explanation for them. The doctors thought it might be leukemia and performed more tests. Something seemed terribly wrong. I feared that whatever sickness my father had, the doctors couldn't fix it. I wanted him well again — even if it meant that he would spend every night at the firehouse, I wanted my old dad back.

By the third weekend in March, we still waited for a definitive diagnosis. Winter had sulked long and heavy for months.

But that Saturday, temperatures soared into the fifties. The wet, fertile scent of spring wafted in the breeze—we longed to shed our winter coats and heavy bedspreads, ready to start over again, with the hope that my father would be fine. That night, my mother washed dishes in the kitchen while my dad calculated numbers for a new tanker truck for the firehouse. He had tuned the radio to Dick Bartley's *American Gold* syndicated oldies show.

When the opening drums of "Don't Worry Baby" by the Beach Boys played, my dad stood from the dining room table, walked into the kitchen, and put his hands on my mother's hips. She turned and smiled. They danced close and slow—careful not to waltz into the refrigerator or the counter.

"Listen to this song," my dad said. " 'Don't worry, baby. Everything will turn out all right.' "

My mother looked up at my father, stood on her toes, and kissed him.

A week later, I woke to a rainstorm pattering the roof. I walked into the living room, ready to watch Saturday morning cartoons, but saw that my mother sat on the couch, tall and stiff. She looked worried. Nena sat on my father's La-Z-Boy and asked me to sit on her lap. My grandmother's green Jeep sat in our driveway and the world outside looked gray and foggy. For a while, nobody spoke.

Finally, Nena said, "Jay, we have to talk to you about something."

My mother cleared her throat. "The doctors had to put a

needle into your father's hip and take out some of the marrow inside of his bone," my mother said. She stopped and held a hand over her mouth, as if ready to cry.

Nena squeezed her arm around me. Just a few minutes earlier, all I had wanted to do was watch television. I couldn't understand what was happening or why they seemed so upset.

My mother looked at me, her eyes hard and scared. "Your father has cancer, and he's very sick. He has multiple myeloma. It's in his bones."

Cancer. The word seemed to seep through my skin, numbing my body. It must be a mistake, I thought. Someone like my father could never get cancer.

"Are they sure?" I asked.

"They're sure," Nena said.

"How could he get cancer?"

"We just don't know how people get cancer," she said.

My dad had just moved us into this new house, *his* new house. He was barely thirty-two years old. People that young didn't get cancer. I had heard stories about great-grandparents, aunts and uncles, and people in McVeytown who had cancer. All of them had died.

"But he's going to be okay," I said. I squeezed Nena's hand. "Right?"

Nena nodded and pursed her lips. "We have to put faith in God that he will be. And his doctors. He has very good doctors."

My mother explained that my dad would be in the hospital for the next week receiving chemotherapy that would kill the cancer. The chemo would make his hair fall out, she said, and it would also make him sicker than he had been before.

"But then how does he get better?" I asked.

My mother patted her fingertips together. "He has to be strong. He has to fight. He might have to get chemotherapy for a year."

"But you have to be strong too," Nena said. "Your father will need you to be strong."

I turned to Nena. Tears welled in her eyes. Cancer. The word still pounded through my chest. But it was like my father said: "Don't worry, baby."

"I'll be strong," I said. I turned to my mother. "Can I watch cartoons now?"

I turned on the television and my mother and Nena cried.

Part Three

Fifteen

I'm typing a story about the upcoming Pennsylvania Farm Show when my phone rings. The caller is a woman who sounds old and angry.

"What's your name?" she asks.

"Jay Varner."

"Well, Jay Varner, I have subscribed to the *Sentinel* for over thirty years," she says.

I lean back in my chair, ready to get an earful from this woman.

"I think it's awful that your paper stopped printing obituaries," she says.

"We haven't stopped," I say.

She pauses for a moment. I can tell that she's getting more

flustered. "Well, I haven't seen any obituaries in the paper for the past three days."

"No one died. Just as soon as they do, I promise you'll know about it."

The woman sighs, sounding disappointed and impatient. "Fine. I'll just check tomorrow."

Somehow, I understand her frustration. When the scanner sounds on my desk, I sit at rapt attention, hoping for another fire. Each afternoon, I pore over the obituaries and faxes from the local police, hoping the names will correspond and I'll have a front-page homicide story.

The worst part about the job isn't the $8.75 an hour that I earn or the 3–11 p.m. shift that ruins any chance to see my friends throughout the week. The worst part is the death. I glee-fully listen as two veteran state troopers try to one-up each other with horror stories. They tell of discovering bloated bodies — at the slightest touch, the corpses popped open like soda cans and spewed gas. They both remember witnessing their first autopsy. Stand behind the fan in an autopsy, they warn me; if you stand down wind, you'll vomit three seconds after the first cut, be-cause it will be the worst smell you can imagine. And don't wear any good clothes — the smell of death will never come out, no matter how many times you wash them.

Death becomes a daily expectation, a constant in my life. One night, I type sixteen obituaries. People die in their nursing-home beds, in their favorite recliner, on emergency-room gurneys. They die while driving drunk; they stab each other over drugs; they suck on shotgun barrels and blow their heads apart.

One man kills himself on the railroad tracks. I later hear two of the responding paramedics joke that the dead man must have had split personalities— the train's steel wheels severed him into three parts: legs, torso, and head.

A deaf family of four burns to death in a house trailer. Smoke alarms bleated and neighbors pounded on doors and windows, all in vain.

Many of the dead mean more to me than just a name or a story—I know them.

Chip Lemon, one of Lewistown High School's former football players, gets into a fight at the bar and punches a man so hard it sends him down a flight of stairs. The man lands on his head, breaks his neck, and dies instantly. Lemon then pisses in the bathroom, walks out the back door, and drives home. When the police find him, he's at home, asleep in bed.

There is Carl Black, the twenty-two-year-old junkie who dies in the Lewistown Hotel with a needle in his arm. He was in my twelfth-grade gym class.

Kyle Jones, the schizophrenic who breaks open Glade Plug-Ins and dies after drinking the liquid inside, served in the high school Key Club with me.

Autumn Rucker, twenty-three, is found dead in her apartment with a pile of cocaine on her coffee table and a stomach full of pills. Each morning throughout high school, Autumn sat next to me in homeroom.

Timmy Johns who graduated with me dies of intestinal cancer at only twenty-two.

Sam Martin dies after driving his pickup truck into an oak tree while speeding toward McVeytown. The town's Methodist minister had adopted him while she was in Africa on mission work. We sometimes played pickup basketball games together.

And of course, there are many others whose names I have difficulty remembering.

The two elderly brothers who die when a tree blows over onto their car.

The five teenagers who die on their way home from a state wrestling match in Harrisburg. Their car hits a semitruck head-on. All of them attend the same high school.

The two high school students who commit suicide together on a mountaintop lookout. They shoot themselves in the head. No notes or explanations are found next to their bodies.

My girlfriend, Megan, drives down from Connecticut to visit me for the entire week after Christmas. We met in college and had decided to continue our relationship even though she lives six hours away. We have managed to keep our commitment intact through nightly phone calls. It is only the third time we have seen each other since May.

"What do you want to do while I'm here?" she asks. Her brown hair is pulled back in a ponytail and she wears a sweater and blue jeans. She looks even prettier than I remembered.

"There's nothing to do," I say.

"Do you want to go out to eat?"

"Where? McDonald's? Burger King?"

"What about Jimmy's Pizza?" she asks. Then she remembers and lowers her head. "Sorry. I forgot."

"Haven't been back since he died," I say.

I have to work only one night while she visits. I return home at 11:30 p.m. and tell her about a high school honors student who was accepted to Harvard. She died when she lost control of her car. Because she wasn't wearing a seat belt, she was thrown through the passenger-side window.

Megan winces. "Is this what you write about?"

"Pretty much," I say. "Fun times."

On New Year's Eve, we stay at home and play Trivial Pursuit. I tell her more about my job and how it's beginning to wear on me.

Megan sighs and pats my leg. "Like I told you, my dad said that you're welcome to come there."

Somehow Connecticut seemed worse than Mifflin County. I hated things like the Merritt Parkway and the endless suburbs and strip malls. But Megan also hated the isolation of central Pennsylvania and the stink of cow manure that always seemed to permeate the air.

"I know," I say. "That's really nice of you to say."

We smile at each other but then sit in silence.

The double-wide trailer feels cramped and small. Winter air blasts through the cheap windows, through the electrical plugs. I have hated the place for a long time. It seems that none of the work my father put into the house was correct—things break on a regular basis. One night while I'm at work, a massive tree in our front yard blows down in a storm, missing the house by inches.

"This place is a hole," I tell my mother. "I wish it'd just burn down."

"What's wrong with you? This is our home."

"It's a dump."

"It's our home," she says. "I didn't want this place. You know who wanted it."

"What a surprise that nothing's hooked up right," I say. "He did it all himself."

Trouble has plagued the house for years.

The pipes my father worried so much about burst. We had to hire a man in a backhoe to come and dig them up and replace them.

"Good thing you found it so soon," the man said. "This water would have eventually gone right into the fuse box in the basement and caught fire. Plus your well would have run dry."

One day while I was in high school, the basement flooded and we had to buy a sump pump. I spent the soggy afternoon digging a ditch across the driveway with a pickax and shovel so the water would flow away from the basement. During the storm, the brick walls cracked and we had to prop them up with boards.

"This is what happens when you hire the AARP to lay your foundation," I said.

"I knew those people weren't good," my mother said. "But your dad just had to use them because they were so cheap."

When I was a senior in college, the stovepipe on the wood-stove fell apart while I was home during Christmas vacation. I coughed myself awake and saw that black smoke was pouring through the house. If we hadn't discovered it, we would have suffocated. It took weeks to get the smell out of the house.

At the paper, my mood sinks and my temper flares. The Associated Press picks up a story I wrote about a local man who spent thirty years collecting one million pennies. College friends from across the country read the article in their own local newspapers and recognize my name in the byline. They send postcards and e-mails congratulating me and asking how I am doing. I throw away or delete all of them. Then on *Saturday Night Live,* Jimmy Fallon and Tina Fey make an attempt at a joke about the man and his coin collecting on "Weekend Update." The next Monday, my co-workers smile, amazed that a story from the *Sentinel* had made national news.

My mother sees the story on the ticker on CNN.

"You made CNN," she says. "How about that?"

"What's it matter?" I snap. "It was a fluff piece."

That's not news. Death is news. Death is like a drug. Over time, the regular car accidents aren't enough. The freakish accidents aren't enough. I need a bigger fix. And then I get one.

Four-year-old James Van Ness plays with his two stepbrothers in an upstairs bedroom of a house near Chestnut Street in Lewistown. Their mother sits in the downstairs kitchen and talks to a friend. Another stepbrother, fourteen-year-old Keith Thompson, walks into the bedroom to play with James and the boys.

Keith's stepfather has just taken him small-game hunting. A .12-gauge shotgun—still loaded—rests in the corner of the room. Keith picks up the gun, shows it to the younger kids, and says his stepfather told him that guns need to be cleaned after hunting. For some reason, Keith then aims the barrel at James's face and pulls the trigger.

The coroner's report includes all of the details leading up to the shooting. The muzzle had been less than four inches away from James's face when the gun fired. I read details of how James's head—his bone, blood, skin, blond hair, and brains—splattered over half the room. Some of his teeth had been embedded in the wall. James's little body slumped onto the floor.

I call the coroner's office to ask if the death had been ruled an accident or a homicide. The coroner's new assistant answers the phone and I hear the horror in her voice. She had started just a few weeks earlier—this was the first death scene that she had visited.

"I've never seen a body like that before," she says. "I've seen dead kids in morgues. But being in that room was something different. To see that little boy with just nothing left above his neck. And the worst thing was the smell. He wasn't even dead for an hour yet, but I'll never forget that smell."

After I hang up the receiver, I walk into the restroom and dry-heave. I slide against the wall of the bathroom stall and wish I could vomit. This is what I looked forward to—a little boy taking a shotgun blast full on in the face. Guilt gnaws at me. I wished for others to suffer—for their children or fathers to die, for their possessions and homes to burn up. I wonder if this was what my father had felt. Perhaps he had raced toward fires because it added excitement to his life. Maybe he had been bored by life at home. I sit on that cold bathroom floor for what feels like hours and decide that the best thing for me would be to leave Mifflin County.

Sixteen

The Sunday after my father was diagnosed with cancer, my mother and I visited him at Lewistown Hospital. Though just a twenty-five-minute drive from McVeytown, the hospital felt like it was in another country altogether. Its sterile hallways smelled of turpentine and iodine. Fluorescent lights hummed overhead and cast whiteness onto the glossy floors—it seemed there were no shadows in the entire hospital. We walked past nurses and doctors, many of whom smiled at us and said hello as if trying to comfort us. Machines and gurneys sat parked behind nurses' counters or in hallways.

My dad's room on the second floor overlooked the boiler room of the hospital. Outside, steam and smoke lifted into the evening air. My dad, dressed in a white hospital gown, lay in his hospital bed and watched the wall-mounted television. Machines sat next to his bed. One looked like a suitcase and held two plastic bags full of a liquid the color of cranberry juice. A long tube snaked from the bottom of the bag and fed into my father's left wrist. On the other side of his bed, an IV dripped a clear liquid that led into a vein on his right wrist. Also in the room, in the corner, sat a large machine on wheels, about the size of that massive television Helen and Lucky had given us. I recognized this machine from *CHiPs*—it was a defibrillator, meant to jump-start someone's heart.

My mother and I sat down in chairs next to my dad's bed. He smiled and said he was glad to see us. He said the hospital food tasted horrible and joked that if we wanted to see him again, we had better bring food.

"This stuff is going to fix me right up," he said to me and pointed to the machine with the cranberry juice. "That's the chemo. I have to get it twenty-four hours straight for five days." He turned to my mother. "I called Art and he was going to tell the guys at the firehouse. I hope it'll be okay there without me."

"Yeah, what'll happen to the fire company?" I asked.

"I'm sure things will be just fine," my mother said. "Don't worry about that."

I heard footsteps in the doorway. I turned to see Lucky and Helen. My grandfather strode into the room and jingled the change in the pocket of his pants. He stared at the machines, like he had seen all of it many times before. He stood at the foot of my dad's bed. Helen held Lucky's hand and, for the first time, her mouth was closed, that look of astonishment gone. I hadn't seen either of them since Pap and Nena told me about Lucky's past.

"How you feeling?" Lucky asked.

"Not feeling too bad yet," my dad said. "But the doctors said this stuff will make me pretty sick, make me lose my hair."

"You'll look like Pappy Varner," I said. I made sure to say it loud enough for Lucky to hear.

My father grinned. "I might."

Lucky glared at me, like he wished he could punch my mouth, and then turned back to my father. "Hell of a thing, outliving your own son."

"Outliving?" my mother said. She stepped toward Lucky. "He's going to be fine."

Lucky waved his hand as if wanting her to go away. "You know what I mean. How'd that bone marrow biopsy feel?"

My dad closed his eyes and shook his head. "Most painful thing I've ever had. They jammed a needle through my skin and into my pelvis just to get a sample. Dad, I can't even describe it."

Lucky rolled his eyes toward the ceiling and looked about the room, as if he hadn't heard a word.

It was the first time I'd ever heard my father really acknowledge pain. Usually, if he hit his thumb on a hammer or banged his leg on a chair, he'd grimace and say, "That smarts."

"We just love our new house," Helen said. "It's too bad you won't get to enjoy yours."

"I'll be going home at the end of the week," my dad said.

"What day?" Lucky asked. "I'm going to build a pigeon coop in the backyard in the next week. Got the blueprints all done, just have to buy the lumber. Be nice if you could pitch in and help me out."

My dad stared at Lucky and then smiled. "Yeah, we'll see how I feel."

"Do you think the fire department will be okay?" Helen asked. "You'll still be the fire chief?"

My mother sighed and shook her head. "Is that all you can think about? The fire company? What about Jay? What about his family?"

Helen closed her mouth and hand-flattened some wrinkles on her dress. She looked at my father. "Of course I care about you and Jay."

For a few minutes, no one said a word. I wanted Helen and Lucky to leave so that my mother and I could have my dad to ourselves. Before Lucky turned to walk out the door, he looked at my dad, nodded, and said, "Well, I guess we'll see you then."

They left, as always, without hugs, and they didn't tell Dad that they loved him.

My mother and I stayed in my dad's hospital room past visiting hours. My dad asked me about school, if I wanted to go to Hershey Park again this year, and if I had listened to any good music. When it came time to leave, I hugged him and kissed his forehead. My mother slowly walked to his bed. She knelt down to kiss him but stopped. She cried and shook her head, apologizing.

"I'm sorry," she said. "I don't mean to cry. But I just don't understand this. I just don't know why." She leaned her head on his shoulder.

"I know, I know." He patted her back and held her. "We can't think about that right now. I just have to fight this and beat it."

She looked up at him, nodded, and then kissed him good-bye for the night.

"I love you, squirt," he told me. "Be good for your mother."

Before we walked out of the room, a nurse entered and checked the machines. She asked if my father needed anything. He introduced my mother and me. She smiled, knelt down in front of me, and shook my hand.

"You look just like your dad," she said. "I bet you want to be a fireman just like him when you grow up."

On the drive home, my mother and I said little. It seemed that nobody understood how a man like Denton Varner could ever have cancer. I didn't understand it either — people so young didn't get cancer. They certainly didn't die; at that point, I'd never known anyone who had died. It seemed unimaginable. But so did cancer.

"When I had tonsillitis, I coughed up all that yellow stuff," I said. "Will Dad be like that?"

"No," she said. "The cancer is inside his body. It's invisible to us."

"But the doctors can see it, right?"

"They take blood tests and bone marrow. They can read that and see how sick he is."

It reminded me of a fire, the way my father taught me to feel a door for heat. This was what the doctors did when they tested my dad's blood. And the chemo must be like water — it would wash through his bones and extinguish all of the cancer.

When I explained my analogy to my mother, she smiled and began to cry.

"That's right," she said. "His medicine will be like that. And he has good doctors. We just have to believe in them and have faith in God."

If my mother said we had to have faith in God, did that mean we would have to go to church even more? On Sunday mornings, my mother, Nena, and I attended church. My dad had always stayed at home, sleeping late or sometimes helping serve chicken and waffle breakfasts at the firehouse. For the first half hour of the service, we prayed and sang hymns inside a large sanctuary that smelled of oak and perfume. After that, the pastor dismissed the children for Sunday school. Much of church bored me—the songs all seemed similar, and in Sunday school, we only colored pictures and learned parables from the Bible. I didn't like going and I didn't understand why I had to go when my father could stay at home.

That spring, perhaps in an attempt to distract myself from my father's chemo treatments, I decided that I wanted to become a farmer. Both sides of my family had dirt in their blood. My mother told me stories of the summers she spent on her grandfather's farm, helping milk cows and bale hay. She remembered his farmer's tan and how he taught her to shoot an open-sighted .22 rifle—it all sounded like fun. And, best of all, as a farmer I would rarely leave home to work like my father always did.

Much of my inspiration came from Hartley Oden's dairy farm. It sat along Route 522, directly across from Little Brick

Road and some two hundred yards from our house. It had always been there, but it seemed that I never paid much attention until my father got sick. Over the next few weeks, I learned the name of each piece of their farm machinery: the forage wagons, the baler, the hay cutter, the fertilizer, the rake, and the liquid manure spreader, which I called the stinky wagon.

Hartley and his wife, Anna, lived in an old stone two-story farmhouse that rested on a slight hill along the highway. Across their dipping yard, a white, split-level barn held corn and hay bales on the top floor, cattle and milking stalls on the bottom. Two forage silos rose into the sky like pillars, so tall that I could see them from my swing in our backyard. On the other side of the barn, one of Hartley's sons, Dan, lived in a small house with his wife, Patty, and their son, Ryan. Though Ryan and I were in the same grade at school and lived close to each other, we never played together. In fact, my dad forbade me to set foot on the farm. He told me the Odens didn't watch their kids, and I knew that Ryan and his cousins roamed freely, running between the cows and machinery. And my parents told me a story that erased my romantic view of farmers. In 1983, Ryan's five-year-old cousin Jonathan lost his arm in an accident on the farm.

But it wasn't just the accident that made my parents dislike the Odens.

"They're terrible farmers," my mother said. "Don't think that you're learning anything from them."

Most of their machinery looked as if it belonged in a junkyard rather than on a farm. They left their tractors outside all year long, exposed to the elements until the green and yellow of their John Deere tractors turned brown from rust. Their manure spreader leaked liquid dung onto the roads—sometimes the valve ruptured and spilled gallons of the stuff. At least a dozen times a year, either a tractor or wagon broke down in a field or along the road, sometimes sitting there for days at a time until Hartley or Dan repaired it. When I saw that a piece of equipment had broken down, I pointed it out to my mother.

"Looks like the axle broke on the stinky wagon," I said as we drove past it one day.

"They're the worst farmers I've ever seen," my mother said. "They should never leave the machinery outside. That stuff is so expensive. My grandfather made sure that he took care of his tractors and equipment. Hartley Oden just doesn't care."

"Do you think I can be a farmer someday?"

"If you want to be one, sure."

"Just don't tell Dad," I said. "He wouldn't like that. He'd want me to be a fireman, just like him."

Spring burned into summer. It seemed years had passed since my dad had that nosebleed. Cancer had become a white noise in our lives—I could barely remember what life had been like before it. My dad's white blood cells had rebounded—a good sign, the doctors said—but he would still need chemo. Every month, the doctors performed another bone marrow biopsy and my dad came home sore, unable to even sit in a chair, forced to lie facedown on the floor or bed.

During the afternoons, he slept for hours on the orange recliner in the living room, weakened from the chemotherapy. He had taken a medical leave from Overhead Door, but he still mowed our grass and attended meetings at the firehouse. He even went on calls with the fire department, but the doctors told him only to watch from a distance—no air packs, no hoses, no work. And still, no matter how tired he felt, each time his pager beeped, he crawled up from the La-Z-Boy, put on his gear, and drove away.

The chemo was taking its toll though. Most of his hair fell out—what remained looked like peach fuzz, including the mustache he refused to shave. His skin sallowed and his once thick muscles corded. His cheeks hollowed, and his eyes looked glassy and tired. Sometimes he kept a trash can next to his chair in case he vomited after a dose of chemo.

On tepid summer evenings my dad and I sometimes went to McVeytown for ice cream. Ice cream seemed the only thing that didn't upset his stomach. My father would roll down the windows in his truck and blast the oldies station on the radio so loud that everyone in the parking lot of Harshbarger's Sub and Malt turned to look at us. Inside the shop, we ordered two tea-berry cones and then walked outside again and sat in the truck.

As daylight gave way to darkness, the fluorescents outside Harshbarger's flickered to life. At one time they'd been bright white, but years of use had faded them to a dirty, jaundiced color. Gnats and mosquitoes fled the banks of the nearby Juniata River and showered the lights. Sometimes my dad and I just sat in silence, but one night we talked about what I wanted to be when I grew up. He encouraged me to go to college or to a trade school. Above all, though, he stressed that I should do whatever I wanted, whatever would make me happy. After a moment, I decided to test the water for his reaction.

"Dad, do you think I could be a farmer?" I asked somewhat tentatively.

"Sure, if you want to be one," he said. "It's hard work, though. Just be careful you don't end up like Irvin."

"Who's Irvin?"

"Irvin," my dad said. "You never heard of Irvin? Irvin's Hill? Irvin's Light?"

"No," I said. I sat up straighter, intrigued.

"I can't believe that," he said. "You know back beyond our house, there's that hill, about a mile away, where the old shale pit is?"

I nodded, remembering the Sunday drives we sometimes took past that old shale quarry, where only the cement walls of the mining company's buildings remained. It had always looked haunted.

"Well, a while ago, before I was even born, this Dutchman named Irvin lived on Irvin's Hill. 'Course it wasn't called that yet. The guy had a wife and two kids. He farmed the fields up there. One night, Irvin went crazy. He murdered his wife, the kids, and then went to that tree in the middle of the field. You know what tree I mean?"

"Yeah, that big, tall one," I said. "It's the only one there."

"That's the one," he said. "Well, Irvin rode his horse there, tied a noose to the tree, put his neck through, and then kicked the horse. When it galloped away, Irvin fell off the horse and the rope snapped his neck."

Goose bumps tickled my arms. We lived only a mile away from where all of this happened, I thought. "What about the light?"

"Well, the light, that's the interesting part." My dad chewed his ice cream cone—he loved to tell stories this way, relishing his control as the listener anxiously awaited the best part. "When they found Irvin after he hung himself, he was holding a lantern in his hand. No one could figure it out. He should have dropped it. But ever since then, people report seeing a light up there. They say it's his ghost, walking through the fields, looking for the family he murdered. We used to go up there all the time when I was in high school."

"Did you ever see it?"

"Some friends of mine did," he said. "We should go up there sometime."

"Yeah, can we? We could go tonight."

He smiled, happy I had eaten up the story faster than my ice cream. He nodded, started up the truck, and backed out of Harshbarger's. We drove on the curvy back roads, rising quickly over hills and gliding back down. The paved road turned to dirt and my dad slowed down, barely creeping along until we came to a stop. Before he turned off the truck, his headlights washed over that tall tree where Irvin had died. We sat there together for an hour. We didn't say a word, just scanned the darkness before us, looking for light.

On the ride home, my father said, "You know, the Oden farmhouse is haunted too."

"Really?"

My father told me that the house had been a hotel during the last years of the nineteenth century. Travelers could stop for the night, eat a meal, take a bath, and have a drink. One night, a man was murdered in front of a fireplace in one of the upstairs

Seventeen

One Sunday morning that summer, my father stood in the living room dressed in brown khakis and a red polo shirt. He smiled at my mother and me.

"Think I'll go to church," he said.

"Yeah, right," I said. "You never go."

"Well, maybe I should start," he said. "You don't mind, do you?"

My mother's unblinking eyes looked glazed over. "I don't mind," she said. "I'm just shocked."

That morning, we walked into church together for the first time ever. Inside the sparse vestibule, we shook hands and said hello to some of the other church members. Everyone looked toward my father and smiled as if they were happy to be in his presence. Some of them whispered to one another, and I thought that they were probably talking about my father. I looked up at him and tugged at his hand.

"Dad, you look spiffy," I said.

"Yeah? Well, tell your mother she looks nice too. Sunday is the only day she ever wears a dress."

We filtered into the sanctuary with the rest of the congregation when the organ music began and sat down in one of the burgundy-carpeted pews. When the pastor dismissed the children for Sunday school, I stood, but my dad stopped me.

"He goes to the children's room," my mother whispered.

My dad looked at me and winked. "I think he's old enough to sit with the adults."

Until that day, whatever the main congregation did while I was in Sunday school had always been a mystery. What I learned was that real church didn't seem that different from the kids' Sunday school. No one colored with crayons, but the sermon had Bible stories and we still sang hymns.

After the service ended, my parents and I filed out of the pew and back toward the vestibule. The pastor, Rev. Goodman, stood at the door, shaking hands and smiling. He stood tall and straight. His slicked-back white hair made him look wise, but his voice quivered, as if he were weak and tired.

My dad shook his hand. "Great message today."

"Oh, Denton," Rev. Goodman said. "It so good to see you here. We're praying that you get through all of this with God's help."

"Thank you." My father nodded slowly. "It means a lot to have everyone's support."

• • •

That summer took on a kind of routine. My dad slept for hours during the day. Then we went out for ice cream each night, and on Saturdays we listened to Dick Bartley's *American Gold* over the radio. My dad sang along to Fats Domino's "Blueberry Hill" but inserted his own lyrics: "I found my thrill on Irvin's Hill . . ." We opened the windows and let the warm breeze flow through the house — like the old trailer, the double-wide felt like a kiln in the summertime. My father continued to attend meetings at the firehouse and to go out on calls, though he insisted he only supervised. Sometimes my mother pressed him: why did he have to go to the firehouse every day? She said that she worried about his health. My father nodded and quietly said, "Why should I let cancer keep me down?"

For the first time since I could remember, we didn't go to Hershey Park. My parents sat me down at the dining room table one night and explained that my dad was simply too sick to walk around the park for an entire day.

"Dad, you promised we'd ride the Superdooperlooper together," I said, disappointed.

"Next year, kiddo," he said. "Scout's honor. We'll do it. I just don't have the energy right now to spend a day walking around Hershey Park."

"We really wanted to take you," my mother said. Her eyes looked sad. "Your dad just can't do it."

I nodded. It seemed a small trade-in if it meant that my father might get better.

By August, my mother and I were still visiting him in the hospital during his monthly treatments. Each afternoon, we watched *CHiPs* together at noon while we ate lunch in his room.

Sometimes my mother brought him food from Wendy's or Mc-Donald's. Friends from work and the firehouse stopped by to see him as well. They filled him in on whatever jokes he had missed at Overhead Door. Church members and deacons visited him also, leading us in prayers and asking God to cure my father.

Rev. Goodman also stopped by the hospital to see my father. One day he led me to a waiting room so my parents could spend some time alone. We sat on the hard plastic chairs. For a moment, neither of us said a word.

Finally, Rev. Goodman turned to me. "I know this must be hard for you, Jay. It's hard on your parents. But if you ever need to talk, I'll be here for you." He spoke to me like an adult, not an eight-year-old.

"Can God really cure my dad?" I asked.

"Oh yes," Rev. Goodman said. He smiled as if he had all the faith in the world. "God can cure anyone."

"Why can't he just do it then?"

"We pray that the Lord will," he said. He talked slowly and looked me in the eye. "If we have faith and believe, the Lord can work in mysterious ways."

Mysterious ways—I remembered that line from Sunday school. "So, it'd be like a miracle?"

Rev. Goodman raised his arms and looked up. "We pray that he will bless us with a miracle, yes."

"But I don't know why my dad has to go through any of this," I said. "Why did God let him get cancer?"

Rev. Goodman nodded, as if giving my questions serious consideration. Finally, he said, "You can't think that way, Jay.

God allows all things to happen for a reason. He, and only he, knows why things happen on this earth. In the end, many, many years from now, when all of us get to heaven, it is only then that we will understand life's hardships. But you must have faith. Do you have faith?"

"Yes," I said, although I wasn't too sure. My parents did, and Pap and Nena too. Lucky and Helen attended McVeytown Lutheran Church, and though I had never heard them speak of religion or God, I guessed that they too probably believed.

Rev. Goodman told me about some of the miracles Jesus had performed—turning water into wine, healing the blind. I decided that if I believed and prayed hard enough, maybe God would cure my father.

"I'm reminded of Proverbs chapter thirty, verse five," he said. "Every word of God is fire tried: he is a buckler to them that hope in him." He sighed and tilted his head toward the ceiling. "God gives us hope."

"But then why does he make people sick?" I asked.

Rev. Goodman looked back at me. He thought for a moment. "We can't blame God. We must trust that he has done it for a reason. But God doesn't cause sickness any more than Lucifer does."

"Lucifer?"

"Satan," he said. "Lucifer is another name for Satan."

I nodded—Lucifer almost sounded like Lucky. In Sunday school, we had learned that hell was filled with fire and ash. Some of the other kids asked what the devil looked like. The teacher described Satan as an angel of light, lacking flesh and blood, and capable of taking any form. We had been encouraged

to imagine our biggest fear and multiply that by one hundred—
not even that, the teacher said, compared to the terror Satan's
presence instilled. Nothing scared me more than Lucky, and in
some way this connection made perfect sense.

We didn't see Lucky or Helen much that summer. Though
I imagine that they probably visited my father at the hospital,
I never saw them when I was there. I seem to remember my
mother working out some kind of secret system. If Helen and
Lucky visited him at the hospital on Monday nights, my mother
and I simply wouldn't go. They never visited us at home. It
felt as if they cared about my father much more when he was
healthy. It made sense—if Helen had wanted my father to become a fireman so that the family would look better, he must
not have meant much to them while he wasn't healthy.

My dad's doctors had a different kind of faith than Rev.
Goodman. They had been encouraged by my father's progress
through the treatments so far. The cancer seemed to be disap-
pearing. I tried to imagine what the cancer looked like inside my
dad's body, but could still only picture flames burning under his
skin, charring his bones. Somehow, the chemo smothered the
fire, and soon maybe all of it would be gone.

My mother explained that cancer turned my father's cells
against his body. That was why his white blood-cell count had
been so low—the cells are produced in the bone marrow. The
white blood cells protected his body from infectious diseases so
it was important that he have them to get better.

My father's main oncologist, a tall and lean Nigerian-born

doctor named Ricardo Fawcett, remained optimistic. Dr. Fawcett had seemed a kind of hero—my father talked of him with awe, as if Dr. Fawcett were magic.

"Ricardo's going to fix me right up," my dad said. "That guy is good. I've been to enough doctors by now to know what's good and what's not."

One afternoon, while my father and I watched *CHiPs* together in the hospital, Dr. Fawcett walked into the room to check my dad's chart. I turned to my father—he had dozed off in bed. Dr. Fawcett smiled and raised a finger to his lips.

"We can let him sleep a bit," he said quietly. Dr. Fawcett looked up at the television screen for a moment—Ponch rode his motorcycle along a California freeway—and then turned back to me. "Can I show you something?"

He picked up the remote from my father's bed and changed the channel. Two tennis players lobbed balls across the court.

"Ah, this is what I love," he continued. He hugged a clipboard against his chest, as if the very sight of the sport brought back warm memories. "Tennis. Have you ever played?"

I shook my head.

Dr. Fawcett smiled. "Well, your father will have to take you for a lesson when he gets better. It is very good exercise and much fun."

"Can you make him better?" I asked.

"I am trying as hard as I can. So is your father. The medicine will work. He has already improved. I have faith that we can get the cancer into remission."

"What's that?" It sounded like something that should be in a car.

"That is when the cancer stops growing," he said. "It is still there, but it does not keep spreading. If he goes into remission, then your father will be in good shape."

"And then it'll all be gone? He'll be better?"

"Mmm, no. With this cancer, it is never entirely gone. But your father would be able to live for a long, long time." He patted my head and smiled at my father. "Don't worry. He is as strong a man as I have seen."

Dr. Fawcett read over my dad's charts and checked the chemo machine. He told me good-bye and walked back out into the hallway.

Something didn't add up about this faith business. Rev. Goodman had told my father that God would help—so had Nena and my mother. Yet my dad's doctors said that medicine would cure him. I wondered if both could help or just one of them—and if it were just one, would it be God or the drugs?

I still idolized the Odens and their farm. It seemed that I marked the passing of that year by the Odens' field work. In the cloudy springtime, my heart raced at the first sight of their tractors. They sprayed cow manure and fertilizer over the corn and alfalfa fields, readying them for planting. As the film of summer spread over the ridges, I watched the corn grow knee high by the Fourth of July and continue climbing into September. When the green stalks turned brown and dried, they harvested the fields late into the frosty fall evenings.

But I loved the hot days of summer the most; home from

school, riding my swing, watching the Odens mow their alfalfa fields. Pap and Nena bought me die-cast metal John Deere tractors just like the Odens drove, except much smaller. I had pushed the tractors through the house, pretending that each room was a different field. Outside, I pedaled my metal minitractor under the ceiling of oak leaves in the backyard. Like the Odens, I partitioned sections of the lawn for corn, alfalfa, and sorghum.

That fall, under the gray evening skies, Hartley Oden cleaved corn rows in his forage harvester. Strings of brown stalks stuck like flesh in the machine's jagged teeth. When the rumbling engine of the diesel tractor faded at night, I worked on homework at the kitchen table while my mother washed dishes. Outside, the wind rustled the branches of the English walnut tree next to our house, a prelude to a looming Pennsylvania winter, one in which my father would be largely absent. As Dr. Fawcett had hoped, my dad's cancer lapsed into remission. The cancer hadn't been killed entirely, but it was no longer spreading.

"How long can it stay like that?" I asked my father.

"They don't know. Maybe the rest of my life, maybe just a few months."

My father had decided on another option—a bone marrow transplant. He explained that it was similar to a blood transfusion. The doctors would replace his old marrow with harvested stem cells from a donor. These cells would flood and rebuild his old marrow and drive 99 percent of the cancer from his body.

"If I get this done, they said that I could live another twenty years," he said. "If I don't, there's a much higher chance that the cancer will come back and I'll be sick again."

Twenty years was almost unimaginable. It seemed like in-finity—I would be twenty-eight then, my father fifty-one. My father would travel to Philadelphia for the transplant, the clos-est hospital that performed the procedure. Afterward, he would have to stay there for three or four months, which also seemed unimaginable. At least with the chemo, he had only been gone for a week at a time—but months?

Each field that Hartley Oden harvested brought us one day closer to December, when my father would leave. But my dad looked healthier. Without the chemo, his hair had begun to grow back. He began to look like my father again, before the tests and hospital stays.

He hunted buck again that year and this time actually shot one, a beautiful eight-point. I watched as he dressed the deer and cut open the belly with his hunting knife.

"I'll show you all of this when you go out hunting with me in a few years," he said. "But see where I shot it."

He pointed to a small, red hole in the deer's brown fur.

"Right behind the shoulder blade. Aim for that spot. The bullet goes in, hits the heart and causes it to explode. The ani-mal's dead instantly. It's the humane way to do it."

On the Saturday before he left for Philadelphia, he called Dick Bartley, the radio deejay, and requested a song. He sat next to the radio for an hour, waiting to turn up the volume. Finally, Bartley said, "This one goes out to McVeytown, Pennsylvania." This time, my parents didn't dance. My father sat on his chair, tapping his foot but looking forlorn as Merle Haggard sang that if he could just make it through December, he knew that every-thing was going to be all right.

Eighteen

On the night before he left for Philadelphia, my dad hugged me as he tucked me into bed. I squeezed my arms around him and began to cry into his shirt. If I held on tight enough, maybe he wouldn't have to leave.

"This is going to make me better," he said.

"Why's it have to be so far away?" I asked.

My dad looked at the floor and shook his head. "That's just where the doctors are. It's a good hospital."

My parents asked if I wanted to ride along on the trip, but I had decided that leaving my father behind would be too painful. Instead, I wanted to go to school just like every other day.

"Think you'll be okay tomorrow?" my dad asked.

I nodded and cried harder. My dad pulled me close to his chest and gently rocked me back and forth. When I woke the next day for school, my parents had already left. That night, when I returned home from school, my mother told me about what had happened.

Lucky and Helen drove them to Philadelphia, a three-and-a-half-hour trip. My mother spent a few hours with my father in his hospital room and then told him good-bye. He said that he loved her and they cried together.

Lucky and Helen looked on, seemingly unmoved, and said a simple good-bye to their son and left—no hugs, no "I love you," nothing. My father's brothers, Curt and Russ, met them at the hospital as well. They walked my mother out of the hospital and talked about the operation. In the lead-up to the operation, the doctors had hoped that Curt, who shared my father's blood type, could also prove a match with my father's bone marrow.

"When I found out that I didn't match, Erica and I went out and celebrated," Curt told my mother. "I just couldn't imagine how painful it must be to have a needle shoved into your hip."

When my mother told me this, she shook her head. "This is the operation that could save his brother's life, and he celebrates because he couldn't help him."

In the parking lot of the hospital, the Varners exchanged Christmas gifts. My mother watched, thinking about her sick husband inside, wondering how his family could even think about something like Christmas at a time like this. Russ had given Lucky a cassette tape of Christmas music and as Helen's Buick sped along the Pennsylvania Turnpike, she and Lucky took turns trying to jam the cassette into the car's console. They argued and bickered on how to work the tape player. Finally, Lucky threw the tape onto the floor and drove in silence.

"Sometimes I've wondered about your father's family," my mother said. "On that ride, I thought for sure that he just had to be adopted. How could he ever come from such an awful family?"

Fortunately a bone marrow match was found, and the operation went forward. While my father recovered in Philadelphia, Rev. Goodman and some of the deacons from our church came to visit us each Tuesday night. They sat on our couch and chatted about the weather or what they had read in the daily newspaper. Then the serious business began.

"I don't know why he has to go through this," my mother always said. "He's so young."

"God has a plan for everything," Rev. Goodman said. "He has reasons too. We have to put our faith in him that these are the best things for us. I know that might be hard, but he knows what is right for us."

I didn't question what Rev. Goodman said. My mother taught me never to question God's way no matter how unfair his grand plan for us may seem. I was told that one day, and maybe not on this earth, I would understand life's hardships.

"Right now, I believe that he will be healed in Philadelphia," Rev. Goodman continued. "I think that it is God's will for him to be there."

Not long after that, Hartley Oden called my mother and told her that the machines in his basement could save my father's life. All he would need was a piece of hair or a fingernail clipping to exorcise the cancer from my father's body. Hartley explained that his machines offered cures without a single incision or needle prick: my father would no longer be subjected to piecemeal chemotherapy treatments. He said the transplant was a waste of money. Doctors can't be trusted, he said; they only want our money, just like the government. When my mother recounted all this, she shook her head in disbelief and told me Hartley Oden was crazy.

Christmas seemed empty. It was our first holiday in the double-wide, and my mother and I decorated the tree, something my father had always done with us. By Christmas Day, it felt as if my father had already been gone for years. We called him that night and talked. Afterward, my mother and I sat in the living room, not speaking. We turned off the lamps but the tree lit the room — twinkling strands of red, blue, and green reflected off the windows like a kaleidoscope. I turned on the local oldies station and we listened to Christmas music. Darlene Love's "Christmas (Baby Please Come Home)" came on and it seemed the deejay had somehow known to play the song for us. Darlene Love sounded so solemn and lonely as she belted the lines "They're singing 'Deck the Halls.' But it's not like Christmas at all." At the end of the song, her baby hasn't returned.

Just like us, I thought.

Back at school, after the start of my new year, my entire third-grade class made get-well cards for my father. Miss Kaufman, my teacher, dedicated an entire afternoon to the project.

"As all of you know, Jay's father is very sick right now," she said. She clasped her hands and smiled, still seeming chipper. "I thought it might be nice if all of us could make cards for him. Jay, what are some things your dad might like on a card?"

"He likes fire trucks," I said. "He's the fire chief. His favorite color is red and he listens to old songs. And he likes Dalmatians."

I thought for a few moments. My best friend sat next to me and I could recite every television show, movie, and band that he liked. But not so for my father — suddenly it seemed that I barely knew him. When he came home, I promised myself to make him do things with me. I would hide the keys to his truck so he couldn't leave; I'd tie his boot strings together.

At school, my friends, teachers, and school secretaries asked about him. One of the teachers, Mrs. Fagen, a special education teacher I had never spoken to, stopped me in the hall. She knelt next to me and talked softly and gently.

"How is your father doing?" she asked. "You tell him that everyone is thinking of him. We're keeping him in our prayers. And I know the fire company can't wait for him to return."

Though I knew that was true, my mother and I also wanted him back home with us. I didn't understand why the teacher wasn't more concerned for my mother and me.

Someone placed a sign in front of the McVeytown firehouse: THINKING OF DENTON AND HIS FAMILY.

On my first trip to Philadelphia to see my father, I carried in my backpack the cards my classmates had made. I rode in the back of Art Kenmore's Cavalier — he had taken a vacation day from

Overhead Door to drive my mother and me. Near Harrisburg, I saw some signs for Hershey Park. I remembered my father's promise of riding the Superdooperlooper with me. We drove on the Pennsylvania Turnpike for miles and finally merged onto the expressway. We sped along the river and toward the massive Philadelphia skyscrapers. It seemed hard to believe that this city and McVeytown were in the same state.

My mother tried to visit my dad every week but had to find someone to take her each time. The heavy traffic near Philadelphia scared her—her tiny Chevette would never have kept up with the cars racing along the Schuylkill Expressway, plus she had never driven through a city before. Sometimes Pap took a day off from the prison and drove her and my grandmother. Other times her brother, Jed, or Lucky and Helen drove my mother. Before she left, I always told her to hug my father for me.

Art thought he knew a shortcut to Hahnemann University Hospital. We drove deeper and deeper into the city, past the Liberty Bell, past homeless men who wanted to wash our windows. My mother looked at a map and realized we were lost. While Art circled Chinatown, smoke and steam spewed from under the hood of the car. He parked along the street and popped the hood. The radiator hose had burst. He closed the hood, looked across the street, and saw a restaurant.

"Maybe they can help me out," he said.

My mother and I waited in the car, the doors locked. Finally, Art ran back across the street with a wad of duct tape wrapped around his hand. He opened the hood again and taped the hose.

"Where did you get that?" my mother asked.

"In the bathroom," he said. "This was wrapped around one of the pipes on the toilet." He slammed the hood of his car and smiled. "It was all I could think to do."

Art told my father the story when we got to the hospital. My dad laughed and said, "You're a regular MacGyver. I bet that bathroom is probably flooded now."

My father looked thinner than ever. He explained that the transplant nearly killed him. The new stem cells depleted his white blood cells to almost nonexistence. Slowly, they would rebuild, and that meant the new cells would fill his bone marrow as well.

"Getting better," he said. He adjusted his shoulders, looking uncomfortable on the hospital bed. "Little ways to go before I'm good as new again."

"Dad, can you take me fishing this year?" I asked. I remembered the promise I had made to see my father more.

"I'll try," he said. "We'll see how I feel. But we should go out. It'd be fun. Maybe you could go with Art?"

"I want to go with you."

Art smiled at my father. He nodded and said, "A boy should go with his father."

My father rubbed a hand through my hair. "Okay, when I feel better, I promise that I'll take you."

"That'd be great," my mother said.

I laid my backpack on his bed and gave my father the get-well cards. My classmates had drawn pictures of fire trucks, Dalmatians, smiley faces, and rainbows.

When my dad finished reading them, he smiled. It seemed

that he knew just how important he was to my mother and me and to McVeytown. Finally, he said, "Teena, maybe you and Jay want to go to the cafeteria and get some food."

"I don't feel like I even want to let you out of my sight," she said.

"Jay's probably hungry," he said. "Besides, Art and I should talk about some fire-company stuff. Don't want you two to get bored by a couple of firemen."

My mother stared at my father. Her face hardened and I could tell she was hurt.

"Just for a few minutes," my dad said. "Besides, it'll be good for me. It'll help me get back to normal, you know?"

As my mother and I ate hamburgers in the cafeteria, I asked her why my father still had to fight fires. "Could it make the cancer come back?"

"I don't know," my mother said. "I wish he wouldn't. But I always wished that."

"Can't we make him stop somehow?"

"It's who your father is," she said. "He doesn't know anything else."

The doctors in Hahnemann were some of the best oncologists in the country. None of them knew exactly why cancer had formed inside my father's bones. Their best guess had been the years of fighting fires and breathing in the chemical-laden smoke. By the time my father was diagnosed, he had already spent half of his life as a fireman.

Years later, my mother told me another theory about the disease. Some people believed stress caused his cancer, though there was no medical proof that this was true. My father carried

Lucky's legacy on his shoulders like one of those SCBA units he wore at fires — it weighed upon him.

In March, two weeks before my father returned home from Philadelphia, the Oden's barn caught fire. Dan Oden had driven a tractor into the barn to grind ears of corn into feed for the cattle. A spark flew from the tractor's engine and landed in some dry hay bales. Within minutes, the entire top floor of the barn was in flames.

When I rode past the scene in the school bus that afternoon, dozens of fire trucks surrounded the farm — that top floor had been completely destroyed. Black, smoking rubble remained. The other kids on the bus rushed to windows, pressing their hands against the glass.

The first floor, which held the milking stalls and some of the cattle, had survived because it had been built from cinder block and concrete. It now resembled those burned walls of the house in which Lucky had kept his pigeons.

Two days later, Amish and Mennonite neighbors arrived at the farm early in the morning. They had brought lumber, nails, and hammers, offering to rebuild the barn at no charge. It was their way of helping the community, of supporting other farmers. My mother and I watched the barn raising with Pap and Nena — we sat in their front yard and ate a picnic lunch. We said little, in awe of the men's work ethic and their speed. By midafternoon, the crew of three dozen men had rebuilt the entire barn.

I wondered if that barn would have burned if my father hadn't been in the hospital. Without their fire chief, I wondered how the McVeytown Volunteer Fire Company could survive — my dad seemed integral to its existence. I wondered if someone else stopped at the firehouse each afternoon like my father had. And I thought back to the day my dad saved the presents when our neighbor's house caught fire. Maybe if he had led his firemen at the Odens' barn, they would have saved everything.

It seemed that everyone waited for my dad's return. My mother marked each passing day that month with an *X* on the kitchen calendar. He had been absent for so long, I couldn't imagine what it would be like to hear his voice loud and clear instead of through a telephone line. And it seemed impossible that my father would once again sit at our table for dinner or in his recliner in the living room. I didn't even care if he left for the firehouse like he always had — I just wanted him back home in McVeytown.

Still, I understood that when he came back, our lives wouldn't be like before. My mother warned that my father would still be tired — the transplant had taken a lot out of him. It would be weeks before he could return to work, and the firehouse would be off limits as well, at least according to the doctors. My father would need to sleep a lot and slowly ease back into his regular life.

A few days before he returned home, my mother tied a yellow ribbon around the English walnut tree in our front yard. She explained that Tony Orlando and Dawn had a song called "Tie a Yellow Ribbon Round the Old Oak Tree" in the 1970s, about a man returning home from prison who asked his girlfriend to tie a yellow ribbon on the tree to show if she still loved him.

"We want your dad to know that we still love him," my mother said. "And that we missed him."

The night before he came home, I barely slept at all, anticipating hearing my father's voice in the house again. He had promised to take me fishing. And we would return to Hershey Park and ride the Superdooperlooper together. Things would be different.

Pap drove my mother and me to Philadelphia to bring my father home. As we approached the city, I was no longer in awe of its size—instead, it looked menacing, an evil place that had trapped my father for months. I hoped that I would never have to return there.

My dad sat on the edge of his hospital bed, waiting for us to come through the doorway. He looked healthier than the last time I saw him, though his skin was still pasty and his hair looked like brown fuzz. He smiled and seemed to have more energy.

"It's about time," he said. "I was ready to come home about three months ago."

My mother walked him into the bathroom and helped him change from his white hospital gown. When he came out, he wore a flannel shirt, blue jeans, and his steel-toed boots. He sat back down on his bed and sighed.

"I'm still pretty tired," he said. "The doctor said that I had to take a wheelchair to the car."

My mother pushed him down the hallways, into elevators, and toward the car. It seemed that our walk took hours—I just couldn't wait until we were all home again.

At the car, my dad stood up from the wheelchair. He looked

fragile and a bit unsteady. He turned and stared at the hospital for a minute. Finally, he looked down at me and said, "Let's go home, kiddo."

He slept for most of the ride back to Mifflin County. Mom and I, and even Pap, who was driving, kept looking at my father. It felt almost unbelievable. It felt as though if we let him out of our sight, he might be gone for another four months. As we entered McVeytown, my mother pointed out a yellow ribbon on a telephone pole. Soon, we saw yellow ribbons on highway signs, trees, and on the front doors of people's homes. A sign in front of the firehouse read WELCOME HOME, CHIEF.

My dad sat silent, amazed. "They did all this for me?"

Nineteen

On Easter Sunday, my parents and I went to church. People flocked to my father, hugging him, shaking his hand, and just wanting to be near him. The medicine had worked, God had answered our prayers. It was a miracle, just like Rev. Goodman had said—most people did not survive bone cancer.

We sat in our usual pew in the middle of the church. When Rev. Goodman delivered the morning prayer, he stopped and looked toward my father.

"Today is very special for us," he said. "As I'm sure many of you saw, Denton Varner is with us this morning. He returned home from Philadelphia last week. We thank God that he's here today."

A few people shouted "Amen" and "Praise God."

Rev. Goodman raised a hand toward my father. "Denton,

I understand there is something you would like to say to the congregation."

My dad stood, clasped his hands behind his back, and cleared his throat.

"I can't thank everyone enough," he said. "Your prayers for me, for Jay and Teena, the cards and love that everyone here gave me, were incredible and humbling."

He lowered his head and swallowed. "I know you might not think this is the place, but I heard a joke and I think it's appropriate to tell about my, uh, about our situation here. There's a man who hears that a flood is coming. He goes outside and someone in a car stops. They say, 'Hey buddy, better get in this car, there's a flood coming.' The guy says, 'I'm not worried. God will save me.' A few hours later, the water's rising and it's up to the man's shoulders. Another a man comes through, this time in a boat. He tells the guy to get in, but he refuses. 'I'm not worried. God will save me.' Well, now it's really raining. The guy climbs onto the roof of his house. A helicopter comes, throws down a rope, and they tell the guy to climb inside. The guy shakes his head and says, 'No, God is going to save me.' Well, wouldn't you know it, but the guy drowns. He gets to heaven and he meets up with God. He says, 'God, I had faith this whole time that you were going to save me. Why didn't you?' God smiled and said, 'I tried. I sent a car, a boat, and a helicopter. What more do you need?'"

Everyone laughed, some even applauded. Rev. Goodman smiled and nodded.

"The point is," my father said, once the laughter stopped, "I was that guy. No matter what, I believed God would help me.

Of course, the guy in the story didn't take all the opportunities that came along. And I know that sometimes my priorities haven't quite been right. But I learned a lot from going through this, much of it from people here. And I'm not going to get distracted from the important things in life again. It's too short for any of that."

In the weeks that followed, his strength returned. He gained weight, more than he ever had — the doctors gave him steroids to bulk up and regain his appetite. His hair grew back — it was very thin, but there was almost enough to cut. And he returned to the firehouse, leading meetings and taking care of business, just like before. But he didn't go out on calls. Sometimes he even turned off his pager while he slept in the afternoons. I wondered if what he had said in church was actually true. It seemed my father was becoming like one of those dads my friends at school talked about.

On my birthday, we visited Lucky and Helen as always. My mother and I had hardly seen them since they moved to McVeytown. While my father was in Philadelphia, they hadn't stopped by to see us at all. And when my father returned home, they waited for him to visit them.

When we pulled into their driveway, I realized that I hadn't even stepped foot inside their new home yet. The two-story white house sat just yards from the highway. My parents and I walked across the yard. Every time an eighteen-wheeler passed, I could feel the rumble in my stomach. It felt like the trucks would drive right off the road and run us over.

Helen and Lucky stood on their back porch, which led to a sloping yard and then the banks of the Juniata River. Lucky folded his arms, looking as if he already wanted to go back inside and read one of his pigeon magazines—I heard his birds cooing in the coop he had built for them. The small building sat underneath a few elm trees. Helen, standing next to him, waved and smiled.

Another eighteen-wheeler roared past and I tensed up, inching closer to my father for protection.

"Happy birthday," Helen said.

Lucky walked down the porch steps and grabbed my biceps. "Come with me."

I squirmed out of his grasp. "Why?"

My mother stepped forward, ready to protect me. "What are you doing?" my mother said. She looked at my father, worried and angry.

"Just wait," my father said. He patted her shoulder. "Hold on, you'll see."

"Dad?" I asked.

He smiled and knelt in front of me. "Go with Pappy. He wants to show you something."

Lucky yanked my arm again and we walked across the yard. Weeds grew against the base of the house—it looked like Lucky never used a Weed Eater or trimmed around any of the trees. A truck hummed and rattled on the highway next to us. I felt the warm air blow over my face. The air was thick with diesel fumes.

I wondered where he was taking me, and even though my

father had told me to go, I was unsure. Maybe Lucky wanted to show me his pigeons. Or maybe he was going to throw me in the river—Helen had wanted me to get swimming lessons for several years now. Finally, we stopped by an azalea bush.

"What's that?" I asked.

A bicycle leaned against the tree. It was a twenty-inch, with new tires and polished chrome spokes. My heart thumped hard—this was my birthday present.

"I found this bike along the highway," Lucky said. "Must have fallen off a truck or something. I thought maybe you'd want it."

"You found it?"

He huffed and shook his head. "Do you believe everything? It was a joke. Your grandmother and I got it for you for your birthday. You want it or not?"

"Sure," I said. "Yeah. Thanks, Pappy."

He nodded and grabbed the handlebars. "Sit on it. See how it feels."

I mounted the bike. I closed my eyes and imagined pedaling down hills and over fields. Maybe my dad could get a bike too. We'd ride together.

"Put your feet on the pedals," Lucky said. "I'll push you back to your dad."

More trucks rushed past on the highway, and for a moment, I worried that Lucky would push me into their path. But my dad said this would be okay, and I had to believe.

"Don't let go," I said.

"I won't let go," he said. "Just hold on. Get a feel for the bike."

We started slow. I felt Lucky pushing the bike. I smelled his cheap cologne and the strong odor of fabric softener. We passed trees and moved back toward my parents.

"Pedal," Lucky said. "There's only one way to learn how to ride a bike."

The bike started to wobble. I looked behind me—Lucky stood in the yard, watching me ride away. My hands squeezed the hand grips and my body tensed. If I turned too fast, the bike might go onto the highway. I continued to pedal and pick up speed. I passed the back porch and saw my parents.

My dad smiled. "Keep going. Keep riding."

"Help me," I said. "I can't stop."

The end of the yard and a line of trees lay in front of me. I slowly turned the handlebar. The bike made a U-turn and I approached my parents again.

"I want off," I yelled. "How do I stop?"

"Pedal backward," my dad said.

The bike wobbled a bit and I felt unsteady, as if I could crash at any minute. I passed Lucky—he didn't even look at me. I kicked the pedals backward and the bike tipped over in the grass. For a few moments, I lay still, unsure of what had just happened.

"What did you do to him?" my mother asked. "Did you make him ride that?"

Someone walked in the grass behind me. I looked up and saw Lucky.

"Get up and get back on," Lucky said.

"No," I said. "Don't push me again."

"If you don't get on it again, you'll never learn to do anything."

"Leave me alone," I said. "I want Dad to teach me."

That night, my father walked the bike onto our driveway. The sun had already set and the sky looked milky.

"The important thing is to not be afraid," he said. "Just because you fell off doesn't mean anything. You have to get back on and just keep going."

For a few minutes, my father pushed the bike. I experimented with turning the handlebars, judging how far the bike would move. Finally, my father let go and I pedaled fast. This time, I felt like I was in control. I turned the bike with confidence, sharply and quickly, and rode back toward my father.

"I'm doing it," I said. "I'm doing it!"

We finally went to Hershey Park in July, and my dad and I rode the Superdooperlooper together—twice in a row. We laughed and screamed as the coaster twisted around turns and careened down dips and hills. Afterward, my mother bought my father and me matching pins that read I SURVIVED THE SUPERDOOPER-LOOPER! In the evening, we rode the Giant Wheel, like always, our last ride of the day. My mother took a picture of my father and me sitting next to each other, smiling.

She sat next to my father and leaned her head on his shoulder.

"This has been nice," she said.

"What do you mean?" he asked.

"How much time you've spent with us," she said. "I wish it had happened for a different reason, but it happened."

One night the next week, my dad came home with a maroon Zebco fishing rod. I held it in my hand, felt its weight, imagined casting the line into a creek.

"Aren't you going to say anything?" he asked.

"Thank you," I said. "Thank you. When can we go?"

"I was thinking maybe tomorrow? How's that sound?"

"It sounds great," I said. I shook my head and hugged him. "This is so great, Dad. Thanks."

The next morning, my mother made us ham sandwiches and packed cans of Mountain Dew in a cooler for my father and me. He laid the rods on the bed of his truck along with his tackle box. We drove to Kline's Market in McVeytown. Next to the lunch counter, they sold wax worms, earthworms, and hooks for fishing. My dad bought two Styrofoam cups full of moist dirt and red worms.

The man behind the counter smiled. "Where are you two going fishing?"

"Little ways up past our house," my dad said.

"That's great, Denton. Seems like you're feeling better."

"Getting there. How much do I owe you for these worms?"

The man laughed and turned away, walking toward the sink in the back of the store. "Didn't you see the sign out front? They're free today."

"Come on," my dad said.

The man shook his wet hands in the sink and looked at me. "Just make sure you catch something."

My father turned off the highway and drove over a gravel road. He parked and handed me my fishing rod, and I followed him down a narrow trail along a bustling stream. The water hissed and bubbled.

"See how the water's dark in that spot," he said. "That's where the fish will be."

"Really?"

"Yep. They like dark water. It's cool for them in there."

He placed a sinker on my line and a worm on my hook. He handed me the rod.

"Just drop it right into that spot," he said.

I followed his instructions and then sat down on the bank next to him. His rod still lay on the ground.

"Aren't you going to fish?"

"I've caught plenty of fish," he said. "You need to catch one."

His pager sounded. Loud beeps and tones. My dad stared ahead and looked as if he was holding his breath, waiting for the dispatcher's voice.

"Two-vehicle crash on state route one zero three," the dispatcher said. "Caller reports debris in the roadway just past Fisher's Store."

My dad grabbed the rod from my hands and quickly reeled in the line.

"Dad?"

The dispatcher continued. "One vehicle is on its roof with multiple occupants still inside. Other vehicle left the roadway and traveled down an embankment near the Juniata River. Their conditions are unknown."

"Come on," he said. He grabbed his tackle box and rod and then ran down the dirt path toward his truck. He tossed our gear into the back of his truck.

"Are you going?" I asked. "I thought you quit going."

"Jay, someone might be hurt," he said. "Don't you want me to help them?"

He gunned the gas and the truck fishtailed on the gravel

road. He flipped a switch on his dash and the siren wailed under his hood.

"Buckle up," he told me.

When we pulled onto the highway, I looked at the speed-ometer—eighty miles per hour. We veered around cars in our lane. I held on to the dashboard, too scared to feel sad that our day together, our first time fishing together, had been ruined.

"It's the middle of the day," he said. "A lot of guys will be at work. They can't go out on calls, so I have to do this. We'll go fishing sometime later this week."

He pulled into our driveway and slammed the brakes. "See you later," he said. "Tell your mother where I'm at."

When I closed the door, he sped away. I stood in the yard until I no longer heard his siren. My mother walked outside with a basket of laundry to hang on the clothesline.

"What happened?"

"Dad," I said. Tears streamed down my cheeks. "He had a call. He left."

In early August, he returned to Overhead Door, working only half days but slowly getting back to his normal life nonetheless. At the start of August, he bought a new Chevrolet Blazer—or, at least as new as he could afford: a 1985 model with seventy thousand miles. His truck had broken down for good. A few days later, he drove us to State College for some back-to-school shopping. As we crested a hill going into town, he pushed hard on the gas and sped up. The engine roared.

"What's the matter?" my mother asked.

"I'm gonna be sick," he said.

He swung the Blazer into a parking lot, opened his door, and vomited onto the pavement. Next to us, a woman sat in her car; she had seen all of it. She looked repulsed and shook her head, disgusted. My father saw her too.

"Guess I made her upset," he said. "If she only knew what I've been through."

He shifted the Blazer into gear and pulled back onto the road. My dad thought the steroids might have upset his stomach. Or maybe he had just eaten something that didn't agree with him.

A few days later, during one of his routine checkups, his blood work showed low white blood cells again. Perhaps it was the medications, the doctors said. They gave him different prescriptions and ordered a bone-marrow biopsy just to be certain. I couldn't understand why the doctors would do this again — he had just endured the transplant, and the cancer had been in remission before that.

"Can the cancer come back?" I asked.

"The doctors could only get ninety-nine percent of the cancer," he said. "If they find a hot spot —"

"Hot spot?" This was the term he used to describe fires sometimes. Once the firefighters had extinguished a blaze, they would sometimes have to return a few hours later after the fire rekindled because of a hot spot.

"Hot spot means a place where there might be cancer," he said. "But I'm going to be fine. This is just my body readjusting and healing."

Still, I waited in fear for the results of the test. Nothing compares to news from a doctor — when just a few simple words can change everything. Each time the phone rang, my parents and I looked at each other, silently hoping the voice on the other end would deliver good news.

On an overcast afternoon in mid-August, my father rested on his recliner after work. He was flipping through the television stations when the phone rang. He stood, walked down the hallway, and answered the phone in my parents' bedroom.

"Just pray that it's good news," my mother said.

The wait seemed to last for hours. Finally, my father walked back into the living room and sank into the recliner.

"That was the doctor," he said. He lowered his head into his chest and sighed. "The shit's back."

"No," my mother said. In just a few seconds, she seemed to crumple, doubling over, holding her hands to her face, rocking back and forth.

My dad looked at her. A tear ran down his face. "They want me to start chemo again next week."

Chemo. The word lit a spark in me. I bolted outside, mounted my bicycle, and pedaled hard, so hard that my legs burned. I rode through the fields, the alfalfa lapping against my bare legs. Not more chemo, I thought. That meant more hospitals and another transplant. My father would be gone just like before.

"Just have faith in God," I said. The louder I said it, the truer it would become. But I had said that the last time. I breathed harder and felt the anger wash through my blood.

"Just have faith in God."

It became a mantra—I repeated it again and again, each time pedaling harder and faster, hoping that somehow my bike would lift off the ground and I could fly far away.

Twenty

My dad finished out the week working only half days at Overhead Door. He still slept for hours on the couch in the living room, covered up with a blanket despite the late August heat. The stoic defiance he had demonstrated before seemed less potent now — he looked depressed, not ready to muster the will for another round of chemo. On the Saturday before he was to leave for the hospital, his pager beeped while he slept. The tinny sound of the dispatcher's voice gave the address of a structure fire in McVeytown. My dad sat up, swung his legs onto the floor, and tied his steel-toed boots.

My mother walked into the living room and shook her head. "Denton, do you really think you should go?"

He rolled his eyes and stood. "It's right downtown."

"You're sick," she said.

"I'll be fine." He walked outside, stepped into his truck, and drove away.

My mother folded his blanket, sat down on the couch, and then she cried, squeezing the blanket tight against her chest.

"He's sick," she said. "It's not just the cancer. There's something not right in his head. He can't stay away from those fires. It's like he's addicted to it."

My father returned home from the house fire hours later, stumbling as he walked through the door. His legs dragged, as if weight had been tied to his feet. He leaned against the kitchen counter for a moment and caught his breath. Then he peeled off his wet jeans and unrolled his sopping socks.

"What in the world did you do?" my mother asked.

My dad laughed softly. He explained that water from the fire hoses had flooded the basement of the house.

"Unfortunately, the circuit breaker was down in the basement," he said. "We had to get down there and turn off the power."

My father volunteered for the job, wading through the basement with a flashlight while water poured down his bunker boots. He found the circuit breaker and turned off the power. After he finished telling the story, he nodded, as if it were all in a day's work.

"You walked in water to turn off electricity?" my mother asked. Her jaw tightened and I saw the raw anger in her eyes. "Are you stupid, Denton? Did you want to get electrocuted?"

My dad shrugged. "If I didn't do it, it might have blown up. Didn't want someone getting hurt."

. . .

Just before going into the hospital again, my father came up with an idea to breed animals. He would raise pheasants and then sell them. Best of all, my dad said it was a project that he and I could work on together. Lucky gave my father an old incubator flecked with rust. It opened like a waffle iron and had indentations for eggs. My father bought thirty-one pheasant eggs and showed me how to care for them. Each morning and night, I would turn the eggs, allowing them to warm on alternating sides.

He even gave me a demonstration about the eggs, taking me outside and dropping a chicken egg on the ground.

"See the yellow?" he said. "That's the yoke. With eggs like this, it means that a chick won't hatch."

He dropped one of his pheasant eggs onto the ground. Instead of yellow, the insides looked red and pulpy.

"See the blood? That means there is a chick inside of that one. If we keep it warm and care for it, all of them should be fine and we'll have a bunch of pheasants."

"And you want me to do this?"

"We'll do it together," he said. "But you'll be in charge when I'm in the hospital. Think you can handle it?"

"You bet," I blurted. I didn't want to let him down.

In September, he returned to the hospital for chemotherapy. My mother and I visited him the first night. He watched television. The same machines as before sat next to his bed.

"Don't worry," he told me. "Remember what I told you about learning to ride your bike?"

"If I fall, get back on," I said.

"Yep. That's what I'm doing. The chemo didn't work last time. This time it will."

A few nights later, he suffered a seizure while he slept, ripping IVs out of his arms. After that, the doctors moved him to the hospital's intensive care unit.

The ICU hallway seemed quiet and still. Large trash cans with biohazard warning labels on their lids sat outside the rooms. I peeked into some of the rooms—the patients all looked close to death. Machines sat next to their beds; there were hoses stuck in their mouths; family members huddled inside and cried.

My dad looked worse than I had ever seen him. He slipped in and out of consciousness—the doctors wanted to sedate him to prevent any more seizures. We sat for fifteen minutes and talked to him, unsure how much he could even hear. Before I left, I told him about starting fourth grade. I explained that my new teacher seemed kind and funny, that I sat near many of my friends. As I stood to leave, my father's eyes opened.

I leaned toward him, trying to hear his weakened voice. He smiled, weary and tired, and said, "Be good for your mother."

The next day, another seizure hit. This time, he nearly bit off his tongue. The doctors decided that sedation wasn't enough; they induced a coma and my father became unresponsive.

My mother, Pap, Nena, and I all sat in a cold hospital room in the evenings and watched my father lie motionless in bed.

"Where are Lucky and Helen?" I asked.

"They come during the day while you're at school," my mother said. "That way, you and I can visit him at night. We're only allowed to have four people in his room at a time."

Within a few days, the cancer had spread and now burned inside his brain. The doctors slithered a ventilator hose down his throat. Each time the machine pumped air into his lungs, it hissed like a deflating tire. On the monitor, his heart line spiked and sank, bleeping with each beat. IV tubes pricked the veins of his arms. We stared at him until we cried, and then sat in silence until we cried again.

Sometimes Pap took me to McDonald's for supper or to Kmart to look at the toys—anything that might cheer me up. One night he bought me my first watch, a Timex Ironman just like my father's. I had always asked my father for the time and then grabbed his thick, strong arm to look at the digital numbers. When it was dark, I pressed a button on the side that illuminated the face in a green glow.

The next day, I held the watch in front of my father's face as he lay on the hospital bed. His eyes were closed and his chapped lips separated by the white gauze wrapping his tongue.

"Look Dad," I said. "It's a watch just like yours."

The beat of his heart bleeped on the screen next to the bed.

Somehow I thought that trying to be more like my father might bring him out of his coma. Throughout those weeks at the hospital, I had begged my mother to buy me a Honda CR70, a newer model of the same motorcycle my father once said that he had owned when he was my age. But my mother wouldn't even allow me to page through the motorcycle magazines in the grocery store, let alone look at a real motorcycle, always telling me that I was too young for such a dangerous machine.

We continued to visit my dad in intensive care, and each

time, we stood next to the bed and cried. Now, however, the nurses came inside and ushered us away soon after we arrived.

"How come we could visit him so much longer before?" I asked my mother.

"They want to make sure your dad doesn't have any distractions," she said. "Intensive care is for very sick people, and the nurses would rather not have many people in the room."

But a week later, the doctors moved my father from intensive care to a private room. He had developed pneumonia and a tube that looked like the hose from a vacuum cleaner pumped air into his lungs. After what my mother had told me, I thought that moving my father from intensive care meant that he had improved. I looked at my father, unmoving in his hospital bed, and thought that in a few days he would come out of his coma. I would be able to talk with him again and hear his voice.

The next day, my mother and Nena sat in the living room and talked with me. I remembered when they had first told me about the cancer. Just have faith in God, Nena had told me. Now, I thought that they were going to tell me that my father had come out of his coma, that he was better, that God had blessed us with a miracle.

When I asked them this, my grandmother cried. She sat on my father's recliner and her chest heaved so hard that she began to cough. I had never heard anyone cry like this before— miserable, mournful wails.

"They don't think your dad is going to get better," my mother said. She sat next to me on the couch and wrung her hands together. "The doctors did something called an exploratory operation. They wanted to go inside of him and look. The cancer was all through him."

But that didn't make sense. What about the faith we had in the doctors and in God? I remembered the day he learned that the cancer had returned: "Just have faith in God," he said.

"But what about a miracle?" I asked.

The phone rang at 3:00 a.m. on a rainy late September morning in 1990. My mother, exhausted from worry and dread, answered. A nurse from the hospital explained that my father's condition had worsened during the night, and the doctors believed he wouldn't live much longer. In the dark of night, Nena and my mother drove to the hospital to see my dad one last time. Little had changed. He still lay unresponsive in his hospital bed and the respirator pumped air into his lungs. IVs were still hooked into his veins, but they knew now that the machines and medicine only delayed the inevitable—the cancer had poured from his bones like lava, washing through his organs and brain. His lungs had flooded with pneumonia.

My mother called the nurse.

"Go ahead," she said. "Get it all off of him."

She walked into the hallway and held on to my grandmother, crying as my father died. Finally, the nurses came out of his room, nodded, and said that my mother could see him if she wished.

He looked peaceful, she told me. No more tubes, hoses, or

monitors. The long, endless fight was over, and my dad's body had simply lost. My parents had been married thirteen years. They had been each other's first and only real loves. My mother bent down, kissed my father's still warm forehead, and walked away.

Outside, the breaking dawn softened the mottled sky above Lewistown. It rained during their car ride home. Later that morning, my mother woke me—I had slept through all of it. She knelt on the floor next to my bed and held on to my hand.

"Your dad's all better," my mother said.

"Was it a miracle?"

Her lips tightened and tears welled in her eyes. "No, honey. God thought it was time to take your father to heaven. He's there now. All the cancer is gone. He's all better."

In that instant, my body felt as if it had drifted into some kind of shock. I couldn't move or speak. He wasn't better, as my mother had said—he was gone. I would never hear his voice again, feel the touch of his hand, smell the shampoo he used, the smoke that clung to him. I would never again watch him run out the door to a fire. It seemed everything inside of me understood the awfulness of the world at that moment. Somehow, I hoped that I would shut down too—my heart, my stomach, my lungs. Then I would be lifted away from all of this. I wanted to be all better too.

Finally, I rolled away from my mother, buried my face in a pillow, and cried. Everything seemed so meaningless. No matter what, nothing would ever bring my father back.

Later that day, my mother asked Pap to take me away from

the aftermath of death that permeated our house—she had to talk with the funeral director about services and an obituary. So my grandfather took me to the only motorcycle showroom in the county.

As he drove over winding backcountry roads, I saw a camouflaged hunter wade through knee-high alfalfa, a shotgun cradled in his arms. Pheasant season had started the weekend before, something my father never missed. I had watched him hunt in the fields near our house, his fluorescent orange hat a beacon among the rows of dead brown stalks of corn. He had talked about the year when I would turn twelve, when most fathers passed down rifles and shotguns to their sons. A boy's first hunting license was the first step toward becoming a real man. Each year, on the last Monday in November when buck season started, the men faded into the woods for days at a time and it was every boy's dream to follow them.

"Who'll teach me to hunt now?" I asked my grandfather.

He stared out the windshield for a moment and then said, "I'll do it."

In his casket, my father wore a mesh hat, blue jeans, a flannel shirt, his steel-toed boots, and that Timex Ironman watch. These were the clothes my father loved, and I liked that he was dressed the way I would always remember him. Even before the cancer, he had said that he hated it that people wore suits and ties in their graves when they never wore them while alive.

Only family attended the viewing—Pap and Nena, Lucky

and Helen, my father's brothers Curt and Russ. I remember the tears and that I had begged to not look at my father inside the casket.

Nena kneeled in front of me. "You have to tell your father good-bye," she said.

She held my hand and led me to the casket. I was reminded of the day we rode together in the parade—he'd said that he looked spiffy. I leaned over and kissed his cold cheek, and I told him that I loved him.

Afterward, in the parking lot, family members hugged my mother and me. My uncle Curt—the one who had celebrated when his bone marrow didn't match his brother's—told me what a great guy my father had been, how much good he had done for the community. His wife, Erica, patted my mother's shoulder.

"Well, Teena, all I can say is good luck," my aunt said. "Life goes on."

My mother and I hated that saying—in a sense, sure, life went on, but we knew nothing would ever be the same.

Lucky dug his hand into my shoulder like a claw. He looked down at me and said, "You're the man of the house now. It's your job to get that firewood in and mow the grass. You better act like a man now."

I thought of my father's watch while I sat at the front of the church during the funeral. I stared at the flower-covered silver coffin and wondered how long the watch would keep ticking. It seemed unfair that time continued for any of us, that anything dare carry on without my father. At the end of the service, the pallbearers—my father's firefighter friends—picked up the casket and walked down the aisle of the church. When my family stood to follow, Pap leaned down and said, "You lead the way." I stepped into the aisle, looked down at the burgundy carpet, and then walked back through the center of the church. People stood at the back of church—the pews were full. Even though it was a workday, firefighters drove to McVeytown from across the state—they sat in their full dress uniforms. During the procession to the cemetery, I looked out the back window of my grandfather's Subaru and saw the long stream of cars behind us, amazed that so many people had known my father.

I continued turning the pheasant eggs in the incubator like my father had instructed, though my mother declared it a waste of time. I explained that my father had put me in charge of the project—I wanted to carry it out. Each day, I waited for the chicks to hatch. Eventually, though, the eggs began to smell rotten, and my mother made me throw them away. I gathered the eggs in a plastic bag and carried them to that pile of debris excavated from the hole—it still sat in our yard, an eyesore, my mother called it. One by one, I threw an egg at the busted up cinder blocks and rocks, each time throwing harder. I cried as I watched their red and yellow gooey insides splatter. I had let my father down.

Part Four

Twenty-one

Fire trucks, ambulances, and state police cruisers sit in front of the farm. A few firemen and a trooper smoke cigarettes nearby. They look to be silent and all stare off in different directions. Tractors and wagons cluster near the red wooden barn. I know that I am too late—whatever has happened is over, though I don't see any hints of a fire, or even smell the stinging smoke. If not for the emergency vehicles, this would be just another dairy farm outside McVeytown.

Elizabeth reached me while I was driving to the newsroom for my evening shift. Someone had heard a call come over the police and fire scanner that sat at my empty desk: there was a rescue operation under way on a farm. I was told to find out what I could and write about it.

And so I come to this farm. I park in front of a nearby church and walk on the gravel beside Ferguson Valley Road, toward two fire policemen standing at the end of the dirt lane that leads to the farm and those fire trucks. The cold January air bleeds under my collar and onto my neck. What were once mud puddles in the lane have since crusted over with ice. Old stone farmhouses like the one where the accident occurred nestle against the ridgelines here. Holstein cattle splotch the green pastures like ink blots. Forage silos stick like towers into the sky.

The fire policemen wear orange vests and camouflage mesh hats. They look like a pair of hunting buddies on the first day of buck season. Both need a shave. Their lower lips bulge from dips of chewing tobacco. I introduce myself, tell them I am a reporter with the *Sentinel* and ask what has happened.

"Probably don't know anything more than you do, bud," one of them says. His eyes are hidden behind a pair of yellow tinted sunglasses. "They don't tell us shit." He laughs and taps his buddy on the shoulder as if they are the only ones in on the joke.

"They been down there for a half hour now," Sunglasses continues. "Probably be there for a while longer. Coroner ain't even here yet."

"The coroner?" I ask. My heart beats stronger. "Someone died? How?" I flip open my yellow legal pad and click my pen, ready to take notes.

Sunglasses shrugs and says, "Farming accident. Could've been kicked in the head by a cow for all I know. Don't even know his name."

A breeze blows through the scattered oak saplings lining the road. Their branches make a noise that reminds me of knuckles cracking. I look back at the farm that snuggles against the gray ridge. Winter has stripped the trees of their foliage. Somehow, I think that there is a connection to be made between those bare trees and myself. Four months on this job, back in my hometown, have left me feeling just as empty. Soon spring's warmth would draw out blossoms and green the land, yet my purpose of reporting things like this would remain unchanged. I force myself to focus.

"Is there a trooper down there I could talk to?" I ask. In any kind of death investigation all of the firemen are useless except for the chief. Subordinates aren't allowed to talk with the media; I have to hunt out the man at the top, who, on this day, I assume is too busy to answer questions. The next place to go for answers is the Pennsylvania State Police.

Sunglasses walks to his beat-up Chevy Blazer, opens the door, and grabs the microphone on his radio unit. The other man, the silent partner, stares at me, half grinning as tobacco juice leaks out the side of his mouth and onto his beard. He spits a brown wad of juice and says, "They really don't tell us shit. We just stand here like dummies."

I look back at my car and at the church. The steep hill that rises behind the plain white building leads to the cemetery where my father is buried. If I stood at his grave I could spy down onto this whole scene, but I haven't returned there since the day we buried him—and suddenly I don't know why. Many of the firemen inside that barn probably served with my father when he was chief. If he were alive, I'd be asking him the questions.

"He says they don't want no one down there," Sunglasses

yells from his truck. "They're going to be cleaning up for a while."

I think of pushing them for more information or asking to use the microphone and request a trooper myself, but I back off out of respect. "Cleaning up" tells me enough about whatever has happened. I think back to an accident I saw a few weeks before I got this job: an eighteen-wheeler broadsided a small sedan at an intersection near McVeytown. I saw Art Kenmore, now the McVeytown fire chief, sitting on the back of a pickup. He wore only a white T-shirt and his bunker boots. His helmet sat on the tailgate next to him. He stared down at the road as though praying, never looking up as other men walked past, as state troopers photographed the scene. A white sheet covered the wrecked car and, as I later read in the newspaper, the woman inside. The force of the accident was so strong that it ripped her head off.

I know that whatever happened on that farm had to be grisly. The firemen and state troopers would not be in the mood to talk.

Later, hours after I have finally come to the newsroom, the coroner phones in the report. All night I have silently wondered where the story would play on the front page. A flipped tractor, while horrible, won't garner the same reaction as a mauling. And even if a cow had kicked someone in the head, that could be played up simply for its novelty. When the coroner tells me what happened, I know that tomorrow everyone will be talking about Allan Groff.

He was sixteen, a Mennonite, and allowed to drop out of

school to help on his family's farm. As Groff poured bags of corn into a grinder meant to mill the food for livestock to eat, a piece of his clothing snagged in the machine's metal claws. No one heard his screams over the roar of the engine. The rotating claws first ate his arm, and then worked their way toward his shoulder and head. I imagine blood spewing from the mouth of the grinder and into the corn. Who cleans this up? What do they do with it? But you can't ask these questions, only the who, what, where, when, and why. I try to fill in the blanks after work as I lie in bed, wonder how much of Allan Groff's body was chewed up and spit out by that machine, if he was already dead when his father found him. Before I fall asleep that night, I wonder how his father could ever walk into that barn again and not think of his son's body ripped apart by grinding metal.

The next night at work, I type Groff's obituary. Sometimes the funeral home directors bring snapshots into the office if the family wants to include an image with the obituary, for an extra twenty-dollar charge. All but one of the funeral directors are men. Most followed their fathers into the mortuary business. The youngest is from McVeytown, the oldest from a town called Belleville about thirty minutes outside of Lewistown. They wear suits, are pissed as hell if we make a typo, and often try to get us to lower the price. My favorite is a man named Roger Barr. He has the finesse of a used-car salesman, the deep baritone voice of a showman, and in the summer, he drives a convertible. He makes death a style.

"Got a photo here," Roger shouts.

I stand up from my desk and walk to the corner of the office near the printers and layout department. This is part of the advertising department, our hated nemesis. To them, the paper is just about money. To the newsroom, it is about reportage. The advertising people are behind the two dollars per line cost for obits—the rest of us feel they should be free.

"Roger, how's business?" I ask.

"Good." He smiles and hands me a photo. "This is for Mrs. Fultz."

Tony, Elizabeth's husband, sits at his desk, Googling golf courses. Since his wife works evenings, Tony often brings her dinner, or just stops in to talk. He is the newspaper's tech guy—he changes the toner in the printers, networks our ancient computers, and designs the paper's website. He stands and looks at the photo.

"That's a good one," Tony says. He is tall and thin and has the deep rasp of a lifelong smoker.

"Yeah, sometimes you never know what they'll give you," Roger says. "Sometimes they give you these photos that you'd swear were in wallets for twenty years."

Tony sits back down at his computer to scan the photo.

"Hey, Roger, what would you measure Tony for?" I ask. It is a running joke between us.

He glances at Tony and says, "Six-two, about one hundred and eighty pounds."

Tony turns away from the computer screen, looking both amused and horrified. "How'd you know that?"

"Experience," Roger says matter-of-factly.

"That's sick." Tony turns back to his computer and shakes his head.

"Roger's just joking," I say. "He's the type of guy who'd hand out matchbooks with 'Thanks for Smoking!' written on the cover."

As Roger laughs, Elizabeth yells my name.

"Alarm codes," she says. "Lots of them. You might want to hear this."

I rush to my desk, turn up the scanner, and grab a pen to scribble down the address. The alarms keep coming, a bad sign—the more alarms, the more fire companies that are dispatched and, thus, the bigger the blaze.

This time, Lorrie drives. I hold on to the dashboard as her white Buick careens up and down the narrow streets in Lewistown. We cross the Juniata River and head toward a trailer fire in Granville.

"If we want a picture, we better get there fast," she says. "With these trailers, they can burn up in a few minutes."

"I know. Used to live in one when I was a kid."

On a flat stretch of road, Lorrie guns the gas. I don't care about any picture. On this cold night, I only want to feel the heat of the flames—I hope it's so hot that I can feel it in my lungs. And I want to smell the smoke—let it soak into my clothes and hair.

The fire policemen stop us at the end of a lane.

"Can't go down there," one says. "Going to get in the way of the trucks."

Lorrie whips the car in reverse and parks along the road.

We walk down the icy lane. The cold wind stings my face and fingers. Over a mile later, we finally arrive at the trailer. A small section of the undercarriage is charred. The firemen are already rolling their hoses.

"We missed it," I said. "We walked all the way down here for nothing."

I find the fire chief, a younger man who shivers in the cold—I notice ice has formed on his turn-out gear, spray-back from the hoses that has crystallized to ice. We talk quickly—a space heater inside the trailer caught fire and burned through the floor.

I turn to Lorrie. "Get any pictures?"

"Not much to get," she says. "But I have some."

We turn to walk the mile back to her car.

"Hey," someone yells behind us. "You guys need a lift?"

It's the fire chief I've just talked to.

"If you're busy, don't worry about it," I say.

He waves us toward his beat-up Chevy Blazer. "You guys will get frostbite out here."

We ride in the tiny bed of the vehicle—his fire gear takes up the entire backseat. He turns his head back toward us.

"What'd you say your name was again?"

"Me?" I ask. "Jay Varner."

"Why's that name sound so familiar?"

"My dad used to be the chief in McVeytown."

He turns back toward the road and doesn't say a word. After he drops us off at Lorrie's car, he rolls down his window.

"I was pretty young when your dad died, just getting into the fire company," he says. "But I remember going to the funeral. Shameful."

"He was a young guy."

The man shakes his head and stares a moment. "That's not what I meant. Would have thought your mother could have at least had a proper funeral."

Twenty-two

A few days after my father died, the *Sentinel* published a story praising my dad's commitment to the fire department. The reporter didn't call my mother for quotes—in fact, the story didn't even reference my mother and me. Instead, members of the fire company talked about my father. They said what a great man he had been, how much he had helped not just McVeytown's fire department, but other companies countywide. The article said that at noon on the day of my dad's funeral, all of the fire whistles in Mifflin County blew for five minutes in his honor, and every firehouse flew their flags at half-staff.

"It would have been nice if we could have been more involved in his funeral," one fireman said in the article. "Since the funeral was on a weekday, a lot of men who wanted to attend couldn't, due to work. And we asked to carry the casket on top of a fire truck from the church to the cemetery but the family made the decision not to do it."

When my mother finished reading the article, she folded the paper and slapped it onto the table. She shook her head.

"A lot of people around here are mad at me," she said. "They wanted a big fireman's funeral for your father. But I just wanted to make sure he had a nice service. He was your father and my husband. Didn't that fire company take enough of his time?"

"I'm glad you didn't do any of that," I said. "I wouldn't have wanted his body on a fire truck."

She wiped a tear from her face. "I don't know. Maybe I did the wrong thing. People wanted to have a viewing. But I remember once, when we lived in the old trailer, your father said he never wanted a viewing. That's what he wanted. And now people are going to tell me that I'm wrong?"

I didn't understand who these "people" were. My father's friends, especially Art, had always been so nice to me.

"Art called me up," she said. "He wasn't very nice. He was pretty smart. He thought it was terrible that I didn't have a big funeral for him, that I didn't ask the fire company to do more. I guess maybe I should have asked them to speak at the funeral."

Still, all of this just seemed wrong to me. Who were other people to say how we should handle my father's death?

"People wanted to have a big meal at the fire hall after the funeral," she said, her voice growing stronger, angrier. "I just buried my husband. Did they think that I wanted to eat a bunch of food? I just wanted to be here, with you. And you know who's the worst about this? Your grandparents, Lucky and Helen. She wanted all of that too. He was her pride and joy because he did anything she asked. He moved them into that house when he was sick. But, oh, she loved him to be a fireman, she loved reading about him in the paper. It made her husband look good, for all the things that he burned." She shook her head and bit her lip. "I can't stand those people. They took enough of him."

The day after the article appeared, Mrs. Fagen, who had been so kind while my father was sick, stopped me in the hallway on my way to lunch. Something seemed different about her—her smile was gone, as was her soft voice. She spoke with a harshness that seemed to bark. And she didn't kneel next to me—she looked down at me.

"Did you see the newspaper yesterday?" she asked. "That must have made you very proud. People said a lot of nice things about your father."

"It would have been nice if they had asked me or Mother something," I said. "And it's no one's business what we did at the funeral."

"When that man was the fire chief, when he was important as your father was, it is people's business," she said. "More people than just you and your mother are mourning for him."

She pursed her lips, sighed, and then shook her head. It seemed that she wanted to say more. Finally, she turned her back and walked around a corner, leaving me alone.

Over the next several weeks, my mother and I saw some of my father's friends and their wives at the grocery store. I didn't know all their names, but I recognized their faces. Each time, my mother stiffened—I couldn't tell if it was out of fear or defiance. The friends usually walked past us without saying a word, pretending not to see us. The firemen's wives were different, though — they stared my mother down, looking like they wanted to pull her hair or spit in her face.

One time we saw Art Kenmore in Jamesway. He walked, next to us, looking down aisles opposite from us.

"Art," I said.

He lowered his head and turned toward us. "Teena. Jay." And then he walked away from us.

"What's wrong with him?" I asked.

"I told you," my mother said. "They all hate me. None of them have been right with me since your dad died."

Not even Helen and Lucky. It seemed as if they had all but disappeared from our lives. It felt like my mother and I were simply tossed away now that my father, their hero, was gone.

That winter, my mother sat me down in the living room and explained that a man would never again live under our roof. Little had changed within our house since my father had died. His blue place mat remained on the wooden dining room table, his flannel shirts still hung in the closet, and my mother continued to sleep on just one side of the bed. It seemed as though his new Blazer could rumble into the driveway at any time and then I would hear his steel-toed boots stomp up the porch steps.

"If you're worried about me getting a boyfriend or stepfather, don't be," my mother said. She was thirty-two then, and thin. Her curled brown hair flowed past the collar of one of those faded flannel shirts that my father once wore.

"I only ever loved one man," she continued. "When I met your father, I knew he was the one. I knew it on our first date."

236 | JAY VARNER

She looked down at the silver wedding band on her right hand and cried. The ring was usually worn on the left hand, she had explained. Wearing it on the right was a sign of loss. "I'm not going on a date again, even if someone asks me."

I didn't know what to say or do that would make her feel better. Instead, I slowly nodded and wished that I had someone to talk to about these things.

"And don't worry about learning how to drive or hunt or use tools; someone will teach you," she said. "Pap will teach you."

When our old lawn mower broke that next summer, Pap drove his tiny Ford Ranger pickup to our house. He reached across the seat, grabbed his toolbox, and then shimmied out of the truck, wincing in pain from the arthritis that caused him to hobble like a bowlegged cowboy. When his wrench slipped or a bolt fell into the engine block, my grandfather sighed and tugged the red and white hankie out of his back pocket and wiped the sweat from his face. After hours of fumbling, bloodying his knuckles, and drinking several glasses of ice water, he fixed the mower so that it ran for a few more weeks. But there was his declining health: arthritis, high blood pressure, a hip replacement. I needed to become a man fast so I could take care of my mother. I wanted to know how to run a chain saw, swing a splitting maul, and replace blown fuses. For now, though, I raked grass and crawled around the outside of the house on my knees with a pair of hedge clippers, hardly the work of a real man.

One night, after we finished working, my mother and I sat on the front porch and drank water. Crickets chirped in the distance.

"I wonder what your father would say about all of this," she said. "All of those guys who were supposed to be his friends, they can't even stop by to check up on us. They don't offer to do anything with you."

"I thought maybe Art would take me fishing," I said. "He said something about it that one time in Philadelphia."

My mother shook her head and looked toward the orange horizon. "Nope," she said. "They don't care about us."

I wondered the same about Lucky and Helen. Since my father's death, we had seen them only briefly. On my birthday they stopped by our house to drop off our presents—Lucky stayed in the car while Helen walked the gifts to our door. For Christmas, they mailed me a card with a twenty-dollar bill inside. Though this should have upset me, ultimately, I felt glad that I didn't have to see them.

Not long after that, my mother and I watched the movie *Backdraft* together. Early in the film, some of the firefighters visit Rebecca De Mornay's character, a widow with children. Her husband, a fireman, had been killed on the job. His friends and co-workers stop by to deliver groceries and check on the kids.

"Is that how it's supposed to be?" I asked.

"We wish," my mother said.

"Well, that movie's not true anyway," I said. "Those firemen, they were running with their jackets open. Dad told me once that if someone did that, they'd burn up."

"Yeah," she said. "I bet real firemen don't act like those guys in the movie."

• • •

At the start of fifth grade, I became friends with Ryan Oden, Hartley's grandson. Ryan and his parents still lived in that small house on the farm. From their back porch I could see the manure pit where a front-end loader shoveled cow shit. A fenced, concrete pad held the cattle, their feeding and water troughs, and several sheet-metal buildings where Ryan and I hunted pigeons. The upstairs of the two-story barn held hay bales and sacks of ground corn used to feed the cattle. Downstairs were the fifty or so milking stalls.

Though my parents had once forbidden me to step foot on the farm, my mother now seemed happy that I wanted to go outside the house and encouraged that I had wanted to do "boy things" with Ryan. But she always told me to be careful, reminding me of Jonathan's deformed arm. My dream of becoming a farmer had faded, but I remained intrigued by the Odens. Harley's machines and the rumored blood-stained floorboards still captivated me. In the summertime, I played basketball with Ryan and some of his cousins, including Jonathan. He shot right-handed while his other arm curled against his chest in the brace. Jonathan worked on the farm too, driving the Oden's old Moline tractor—quickly shifting the gears, then grabbing the steering wheel. He did it all as fluidly as a gymnast.

One soupy summer night, when Ryan and I played tag with his cousins, Jonathan invited me into his room. He lived with his parents in a house a hundred yards from the farm. Baltimore Orioles posters and baseball cards decorated the bedroom along with a baseball that was protected inside a plastic case. I saw the autographs of Mike Boddicker, Cal Ripken Jr., and Eddie Murray.

"How did you get that ball?" I asked.

"I threw out the first pitch at a game," he said. "After my accident. They gave it to me."

My mother and grandmother had told me what happened to Jonathan's arm, but no one on the farm ever spoke of it. This was the only time Jonathan ever mentioned it to me.

"You know, your dad was there that day," he said. "I don't remember him but people told me that he was the first one to come. Because of him I was able to keep my arm."

I had felt cheated by the McVeytown Volunteer Fire Company. Had it not been for that firehouse, I would have seen my dad more often. But now it didn't matter—his body lay buried in a cemetery and I would never speak another word to him again. But it wasn't just the fire company that angered me—the doctors had lied. The promised twenty years didn't even last twenty months. And though I had prayed for my father every night like so many other people, God had also failed me. There had been no miracles.

I handed Jonathan the baseball and he placed it on his dresser next to the cologne and deodorant. I glanced at the reed-thin arm that was held in the brace and wondered why it had never grown or why they had even bothered to reattach it. I wondered if Hartley's mysterious machines could help, just like he had once promised.

Each day after school, I changed into jeans and a sweatshirt and then walked down the hill past Pap and Nena's house and crossed a two-lane highway to see Ryan Oden once he finished helping milk the cattle. We slowly stepped through the ankle-deep cow manure, careful not to scare any pigeons. We ducked under the electric fence that kept cattle out of the barn. We propped ourselves against iron gates and slowly aimed our pellet guns as though preparing for a gun fight in the Old West. The pigeons lined the rafters inside one of the buildings where the cattle were fed. I stared down the sights, aimed at the breast of one of the birds, and squeezed the trigger. The roosting pigeons squawked and fluttered into the air—all of them except for the one I shot, which spiraled to the ground. We bagged the pigeons because we could, because we weren't old enough to hunt deer like the men in our families.

In late September, some of McVeytown's volunteer firemen climbed onto our roof and rammed long poles and brushes into the chimney shaft, knocking out last year's soot, preparing us for the coming winter. A hollow, metallic clang resounded through the house as they cleaned the chimney, a sound that reminded me of a ramrod being shoved down a musket barrel like in the old Westerns I sometimes watched on television.

After finishing, the new chief, Art Kenmore, knocked on our front door. I stood inside the living room well behind my mother and watched as Art removed his helmet.

"We're all done," he said. "Everything looks good."

"That's good news," my mother said.

I looked up at Art, at his broad shoulders and that mustache—it was thick and wide, like my father's had been. I remembered how my father had laughed that night when Art wore the pink bathrobe. And there was that trip to Philadelphia, when Art mended his car's radiator hose with duct tape he'd found wrapped on leaky restaurant toilet.

Art looked past my mother and into my eyes. He held the stare for a moment.

"Well, all right," he finally said. "We have two more chimneys to clean before the night is out."

"Thanks again," my mother said. "It's still a donation, right?"

Art stared at her, shifted his neck as though his collar were too tight. He looked down at his helmet, rubbed a finger over what I knew was a rubber lip around the edge—I had played with my father's helmet enough times to have every piece memorized.

"Twenty-five dollars is the normal donation," he said.

"I'll send it," my mother said. "Thank you."

Art capped his head with the helmet, nodded, and said, "Yep."

My mother closed the door. "They can't even do it for free. All that your father gave that company, and none of them can give us a single thing."

Twenty-three

One of the first men to help us was a burly, barrel-chested mechanic with thick hands and oil-stained sweatshirts. Walter Marrigan lived two miles away and passed by our house each day to and from work at his service station and garage. That winter, as my mother and I shoveled snow after a storm, I heard his rumbling engine stop at the mouth of our driveway. It was the excuse I needed to stop shoveling.

"Need a plow?" he asked. I noticed the thick bushes of gray hair growing untamed on his neck, hair that crept around the sides of his throat and connected with a scraggly, week-old beard.

My father had always plowed the snow from our drive-way with the Case lawn mower. It seemed kind for Marrigan to offer his help, and we were too grateful to decline. After that, he never even asked and returned after every storm that winter.

One day in February, as the school bus crowned the hill before my house, I knew something was wrong when I saw Nena's old, sea green Jeep parked in the driveway. The Jeep had been there the morning Nena and my mother told me that my father had bone cancer, and then, two years later, the morning when they told me that it had killed him.

When the school bus doors hissed open, I crossed in front of the bus and felt the wind sift down the collar of my coat. I kicked my heavy rubber boots against the siding on the house, knocking snow from the treads, then opened the front door and stepped inside. I blinked and waited for my eyes to adjust from the bright, near incandescent light of the late-afternoon sun that burned off of the snow. Finally, I noticed my mother, who was slouched on the dining room love seat, limp as a marionette. She wore jeans and a flannel shirt. She fixed her stare on the ceiling, as though looking above for answers.

Nena sat at the kitchen table, and our Dalmatian, Patches, slept at her feet. Nena stared at me with unblinking eyes that looked flinty and cold. "Sit down," she said. "We need to talk to you."

I shrugged off my backpack, crossed the living room, and sat down next to my grandmother at the table.

"Mr. Marrigan was here today," Nena said. "He stopped to plow out the driveway this morning. He noticed it had drifted shut during the night. Well, he hit your mother's car. It's nothing serious, just a long green scratch along the front bumper.

And when he came inside and told her about it, she asked if he'd be able to pay for the damage."

My grandmother arched her eyebrows and clenched her jaw. She opened her mouth to speak but started to cry.

My mother exhaled, closed her eyes, and said, "He said that he was lonely. That he thought I was probably lonely too." She opened her eyes and stared at me.

"He tried to kiss your mother. He grabbed hold of her—"

"He pulled me toward him," my mother said and shuddered. "I put my hands on his chin and pushed. I guess I pushed hard enough because he kind of fell back. I pointed to Patches and said, 'You see that dog? She's trained to attack. All I have to do is scream.'"

I looked down at our Dalmatian. She was still asleep, so deaf that she hadn't even realized I'd come home.

"He glanced at Patches," she continued, "called me that word that rhymes with witch, and then he left." A tear ran down my mother's face. "I thought I could trust him."

After I had heard my mother tell her story, adrenaline pumped through my chest and tensed my heart into what felt like a pounding fist; it burned up my legs like gasoline and poured into my eye sockets. I often wondered why Marrigan had been so kind when everyone else avoided us. Now I knew.

I wanted to concoct a plan, a way to make Marrigan pay for what he had done. I began to think of which closets held my father's guns: the little .410 shotgun, the .222 and 30-06 rifles were in my closet; the .12-gauge pump shotgun and .22 rifle were in my mother's; and the .32 pistol was in the second drawer of her dresser. I knew how much each one weighed in my hands, knew how to load the shells and bullets. And I knew how to pull the trigger.

"Do you realize what could have happened?" my grandmother asked.

I was twelve, old enough to know about rape and to understand it was wrong for a man to force himself on a woman. I imagined coming home to a nightmare of blue and red strobe lights washing over our house from the police cars parked in the driveway. And the tall state troopers, slim in their black uniforms, would tell me a different story, one where my mother's hands weren't as strong around Marrigan's bristly chin, where she didn't lie about the dog.

"Does Pap know?" I asked.

"Not yet," my grandmother said.

I looked at my watch, that same Timex Ironman: four o'clock. In another hour my grandfather returned home from the prison.

"Are you going to tell the police?" I asked.

"It'd be your mother's word against that creep's. I don't know if they'd help."

The image of my mother pushing on Marrigan's chin glazed my mind. I looked away from my grandmother. Outside the living room window I saw her Jeep. Just six months earlier, the Jeep sat there as my grandmother broke the news that my grandfather needed another hip replacement. He recovered from the surgery, though his gait tensed and he now looked robotic and stiff. I knew he would have to deal with Marrigan—Pap was the only man we had left.

He sped past our house at a quarter after five. I wondered

what he would do, if he'd be like a cop on television and grab Marrigan by the shirt collar, backslap his face, and then work his fists into the man's chest and stomach. It seemed in character; my grandfather was not always the most rational or patient man. When he lost his temper, his face reddened and gleamed bright with sweat.

He pulled into our driveway ten minutes later. I zipped up my coat and ran outside and across the yard as though I were his cavalry.

"That dumb jerk won't stop here again," Pap said. "He won't even look in here again, you can bet on that."

I stood on my toes and looked inside the cab of his truck. His polished 9mm pistol lay atop a white handkerchief on the seat. He glanced at the gun and then slyly looked at me, almost as if he expected me to be impressed.

"Sometimes you need one of these to prove a point."

"You should have shot him," I said.

"No. He didn't deserve that. Not for what he did. If he hadn't stopped —" Pap looked out the windshield of his truck, across fields frosted in snow and toward the gray ridges on the horizon. "You'll learn all this. You grow to take care of yourself."

I nodded, though I wanted to know all of it now; I *needed* to know it. Who else would defend my mother and me? I matured and adapted just like I was expected to. I yearned for my childhood, yet at the same time I wanted to move forward.

I walked back inside the house, stripped off my coat, and found my mother curled up in bed. The light outside had dimmed, and the sky and snow looked bruised with purples and blues. I sat down next to her and said, "Pap told me that Marrigan won't come back."

She sighed. "I don't know what I'd do without your grandfather." I rested my hand on her shoulder but she lay still, silent. Finally, she said, "I wish your dad were still here. He'd know what to do."

I knew what he would have done: he would have called his friends, those men at the firehouse who followed their chief into burning buildings. A group of them would have gone to Marrigan's house, ready to beat him.

For the rest of the evening, my mother barely spoke, alone in an impenetrable grief that Marrigan had helped cement. She made dinner, tucked me into bed, and then, in the morning, woke me for breakfast. After I left for school she drove to Lewistown, received an estimate for the damage to her car, and made an appointment for the repairs. No one in McVeytown even noticed. No one saw the green paint streaking across her car and no one asked what had happened. No one ever knew about Walter Marrigan or how my mother had lied about an old dog to save herself. As before, we remained invisible.

On Memorial Day, my middle school history teacher arranged for me to recite the Gettysburg Address at the town square in McVeytown. One of the town's pastors drove his sedan in the parade and I waved out the window just as I had done with my father. Somehow, though, people seemed less excited than before.

After the parade, I climbed onto the back of a pickup and stepped up to a microphone. Helen and Lucky stood in the crowd. I had not seen either of them in months.

I recited Lincoln's speech and the small crowd applauded. My grandparents walked up, and both patted my shoulders. Helen hobbled a bit and leaned on a cane with each step.

"That was so special," Helen said. "It was wonderful, wasn't it, Lucky?"

"Not too bad, boy," he said. It was the first—and only—compliment he ever gave me. Something seemed strange about him. His lips quivered a bit, as if his muscles were starting to fail.

"I wish your father could have seen that," Helen said. "He would have been so proud. Do you ever think about joining the fire company like him?"

"No. I don't really want to do that."

Helen's smile faded. She nodded and looked at Lucky. "Well, Lucky, I guess we should get going."

As they walked away from me, sadness seemed to wash through my body. I didn't know why. Maybe it was the mention of my father. Or maybe it was realizing that both of them had entered their final years. Part of me knew that they were family, bound to me by blood, yet I didn't miss them and I didn't love them.

Later that summer, I turned thirteen and the Odens invited me to vacation Bible school at their church. We sang hymns, memorized Bible verses, and were told that Jesus Christ was our one and only salvation in life. Though my mother and I still went to church each Sunday, I had begun to dread the spectacle—the nice clothes, the smiles, and the handshake hellos. It seemed there was something more to the Sunday morning agenda than just worship; there were appearances to keep. I only went along to vacation Bible school out of boredom and convenience—it gave me something to do, and Ryan lived closer than any other friend.

One evening, Hartley drove Ryan and me to the church, using arm gestures to signal a coming turn because none of the car's lights worked. He ignored the blaring air horn of an eighteen-wheeler as he pulled off the road headed toward the church. For the first time I was close enough to see that he was short, with leathery skin aged by summers farming under the sun, and white-haired.

"You boys learning a lot at Bible school?" Hartley asked.

"Yeah," we both answered.

"That's good," he said. "The Lord is a powerful man. He can give you everything and then take it all away. He can cure you or kill you."

Or do nothing, I thought, like he had done for my father. As the teachers in Bible school talked about miracles and a merciful God, I wondered why my father had seen none of this. But maybe it was like Rev. Goodman had said: one day I would understand.

In the fall, Ryan and I again hunted pigeons on the farm. One evening, I convinced Ryan to show me the bloodstains inside Hartley and Anna's house. As we walked toward the house, we passed an inground swimming pool with cracks extending down the sides. Dead leaves and old tires were spread over the floor of the pool. Inside the house, yellow wallpaper covered the kitchen walls, and what looked to be a week's worth of dishes sat piled in the sink.

"My grandmother must not be home," Ryan said.

We climbed a flight of stairs and I noticed a cobwebbed chandelier hanging from the ceiling. The house was cold and drafty. Boxes rested along some of the walls, suggesting the family had never unpacked, or had simply run out of space. Everything smelled of mothballs and dust. Yet, as we walked down a hallway, I peered into some of the rooms and saw that many were empty.

"This is it," Ryan said. "Are you ready to be scared?"

He opened a door and I followed him inside.

The light of a gray dusk filtered through the lone window in the room. Ryan flicked on a light switch and then peeled back the carpet. Two faded black blots, each about the size of a quarter, marked the wooden floor.

"That's it?" I asked.

"My grandmother says that's the spot."

The haunted room in the Oden's house that I had longed to see was no different from any other room. As I stared at that stain, I thought that most of the story had simply been one of those great local legends that kids tell each other, like Irvin's Light. The spots on the floor looked old, but they could have been caused by anything—paint, grease, ink, maybe blood. And besides, I thought, could a wooden floor really last that long? Or bloodstains? I wished then that I had never seen that room—it had been more fun to believe.

Ryan turned off the light when we left and led me back out of the house the way we had come in. We were ready to go back outside when Ryan stopped.

"I have to ask my pap a question," Ryan said. "Follow me."

He opened a door to the basement and we creaked down the bowed wooden steps. Hartley's machines lined the walls. LED lights flashed, needles wagged as wild as a dog's tail, and red digital readouts counted numbers. I thought of the respirator that clicked and pumped my father alive those last days of his life. Computer printouts rolled like carpet across the cement floor, reels of secret statistics.

Hartley stepped into the doorway of what looked like an office. He wore green work pants, a white T-shirt, and a black and white train engineer's cap. People throughout the town talked about Hartley and his machines, yet no one I knew of had ever seen them. Most everyone had heard that Hartley claimed the machines could cure my father. They thought he was crazy or suspected that he practiced witchcraft. But this was the man who had driven Ryan and me to vacation Bible school and talked of God, miracles, and faith.

Ryan asked his grandfather a question about milking cows and then we left. Hartley walked back into his office and never said a word to me.

"What are those machines for?" I asked as we walked toward the barn.

"Farming," Ryan said. "They compute how to help crops grow better. But they can also help people."

"How can they help people?"

"I'm not sure," he said. "But it's got something to do with science, mathematics."

Before ninth grade started, Ryan Oden and his parents were forced to leave the farm and moved away from McVeytown. We still went to the same high school in Lewistown, but like most of my old friends, Ryan entered the vocational-technical program—they spent the first few periods of the school day at Lewistown High School and were then bused to the vo-tech school where they learned how to saw wood and dismantle engines. We still said hello when we passed each other in the hallways or cafeteria, but the games of basketball and the pigeon shoots stopped.

At home, my mother and I continued to work like men. We ranked firewood, mowed grass, and shoveled snow. In the summer, I rode next to Pap inside his little truck as we drove over dirt roads on my uncle's farm, looking for dead trees to cut down and then split into firewood. Then we threw the wood onto the bed of his truck, drove back to my mother at the house, and unloaded it. While we cut and split the next load, my mother ranked the pieces into clean, neat rows. When the weather finally turned cold, my mother still wore those old flannel shirts of my father's; they seemed to swallow her like a child wearing adult clothes.

My mother and I rarely spoke about my father. His death almost became a taboo subject, something neither of us wanted to acknowledge. Even at school, I never wanted to mention it to friends. It would be just another thing that set me apart from everyone else. When it did come up, after a classmate or teacher casually mentioned something about my father, I spoke in a hushed voice, as if his death was something to be ashamed of. My teachers offered condolences. My friends looked at the ground, said that they were sorry, and then sat silent, as if waiting for a cue to continue normal conversation. I couldn't imagine how they would react to news of my arsonist grandfather and his jail time. My mother had told me never to mention Lucky's past: "You don't want people to know what your grandfather did, do you?" And so I never spoke of him to anyone but my mother.

In the evenings, I sat at the dining room table and calculated answers for my math homework. My mother turned on the oldies radio station and we listened together. That music seemed to unlock all that remained unspoken between us, a catalyst to get through the pain.

My mother said that the Platters' "Smoke Gets in Your Eyes" reminded her of that stuffy smell of smoke that clung to my father's clothes when he returned from a fire. When the soaring opening strings of Diana Ross and the Supreme's "Someday We'll Be Together" played, my mother rushed to the radio and turned up the volume. I knew that Diana's promise of reuniting with a lover gave my mother hope. And when my mother listened to Freda Payne's "Band of Gold," a pensive look washed over her face, as she gave the lyrics serious consideration. "All that's left is a band of gold . . ."

The Doors' "Light My Fire" was our all-time favorite song. When we heard the surging organ chords at the beginning of the song, we looked at each other and smiled.

"This remind you of anyone?" she asked.

"Maybe he sang this while he burned down those houses," I said.

During my freshman year of high school, Lucky sold his pigeons, and the coop he built for them now sat empty. Not long after, he moved into a nursing home near Lewistown. One of Helen's sisters told my mother that Lucky's mind had begun to fade and that he now sat most of the day in silence. I wondered if he had put up a fight or was simply resigned to spending his time in a nursing home.

My mother and I never visited him—we had enough to remind us of him. The pile of rubbish from the hole still sat untouched, covered with weeds. It had been years since his last fire, but the remnants of his sparks remained visible. The thought of Lucky rotting inside a nursing home pleased me—he deserved to spend his final years alone, thinking about all he had destroyed. Yet I knew that this feeling would have most likely disappointed my father. He never spoke about Lucky with any anger, only that of a loving, obedient son.

Helen continued to visit us now and again. Sometimes, usually on a Sunday afternoon, she pulled her big Buick into our driveway. Rather than coming inside, she laid on the horn and waited for us to walk outside and talk to her. She sat inside her car with the door swung wide open, her cane resting on the passenger seat.

"How's school going?" she asked.

"Fine," I said.

"Do you know where you want to go to college yet?"

"No."

"Do you have a girlfriend yet?"

"Nope."

She hiked up her dress and massaged her thighs with her fingertips. Aside from her questions, I don't remember much of what she talked about. Usually it was the latest gossip around town. Mostly, her visits were filled with awkward moments of silence. Without my father as a buffer, it felt as if Helen had little interest in us beyond any gossip she could spread.

One summer, she offered to take my mother and me to Hershey Park for the day.

"Of course Lucky won't be able to go," Helen said.

"How is Lucky?" my mother asked.

Helen smiled. "Oh, you know how he is."

"I do," my mother said.

"He's hanging in there," Helen said. "He gets confused sometimes. But I told him about Hershey Park and thought it'd be a lot of fun. He wishes that he could go. He always enjoyed places like that."

"He did?" I asked. It seemed impossible that he would truly enjoy anything.

"Oh yes," Helen said. "I think we used to take the boys to Raystown during the summer."

"Dad never mentioned that," I said.

Helen squinted and lowered her head. She thought for a moment and nodded, "Yes, I'm pretty sure we took them. But I'd love to take you and your mother to Hershey. Wouldn't that be fun?"

"Actually, I think Jay's going with some friends," my mother said, lying. I wanted to hug my mother at that moment—she had read my mind. A trip with Helen to Hershey would have been unbearable. I imagined that she would spend much of the day stopping at the food stands. And of course she would interrogate me the whole time.

Helen's eyes brightened. "Oh, you have some friends? Who are you going with?"

"Just friends from school," I said, following my mother's lead. "I don't think you'd know them."

Helen smiled. "That's just so wonderful. Oh, I hope you have fun."

After Helen drove away, my mother rolled her eyes. "Was that what was wrong with Lucky all those years? He was just confused?"

I laughed. "I thought you'd want to go along with Helen. It'd be so special. Just the three of us together."

My mother shuddered. "I'd rather go to the dentist's office for the day."

Each time Ernie K-Doe's "Mother-in-Law" played on the radio, my mother laughed and said, "Oh, I love this one." She always sang along. "The worst person I know . . ."

In the early spring of 1995, I sat under the raining pink blossoms of Pap and Nena's cucumber tree magnolia and watched the front-end loader emerge from where the Odens kept their cows. I was too far away to see the driver but suspected it might be Dan, Ryan's father, who still worked on the farm. The loader sped across the highway and then bounced over the freshly cut alfalfa field. The small and stiff legs of a calf stuck out of the loader's bucket. I saw the black hooves bounce with each bump and rut until the carcass was dumped onto the ground. And then I watched the burial. I saw a man dig a shallow grave with the loader and then drag the calf into the hole and cover it with dirt.

I went into Pap and Nena's house and told them what I had seen.

"That's illegal," Nena said. "You can't just bury a cow in your field."

"What else do you do with it?" I asked.

"There's a crew of guys who come and pick up dead animals from farms. Who knows what was wrong with it? Probably mal-nutrition. They can't even take care of their cattle anymore."

Over the next few weeks more graves appeared—a dozen or so small mounds of dirt. It was close to the end of April and the Odens had left the corn crop untouched all winter. By now, it was worthless. People in McVeytown talked about the family's legal troubles, that the government might foreclose on the farm because Hartley owed thousands of dollars in back taxes. And now their calves were dying too.

In early May, when the days swirled with welcomed warmth, Hartley Oden drove his old Chevy Nova over the alfalfa fields and placed another machine nearly two hundred yards from my grandparents' house. It was the size of a small television and emitted a constant whistle. He knocked at my grandparents' door and apologized for the noise. The machine emitted sound waves that would help the crops grow, he explained. It was a new and natural procedure, he said, but the government didn't want people to know about it. He left the machine to squeal and whistle in the field for three days.

The Odens' farm appeared to be in complete failure. The alfalfa fields looked more like weeds than crops—Hartley's little box machine must not have worked. But by then, the Odens hadn't even bothered to fertilize or spray the crops with pesticides. And the stinky wagon finally broke down for good, or else it wasn't needed—it seemed the cows had all died or had been sold. We continued to hear rumors of a sheriff's sale.

One afternoon near the end of May, agents from the U.S. Marshall's Office and Alcohol, Tobacco, and Firearms, as well as Pennsylvania state troopers, surrounded the farm. The family was given one hour to gather as many belongings as possible; after that, whatever was left fell under the ownership of the Internal Revenue Service. The newspaper printed a front-page picture of the seizure. The ATF agents wore black windbreakers with the yellow lettering of their agency's acronym sprawled across the back. They carried assault rifles. State troopers stood guard—the butts of shotguns against their hips, the barrels pointed into the sky. By that night, the farm would be vacant—the few remaining cows loaded onto cattle trucks and driven to other farms and eventually auctioned off. A state trooper would tell my grandparents to call 911 if they saw anyone from the family step foot on the farm, as they would now be trespassing on U.S. government property. In the years that followed, people still talked of Hartley Oden and his machines. Some called them witchcraft; others said he poured his money into the machines and was too broke to pay his taxes. Most everyone agreed he was crazy. The entire town wanted to pull back the rug like Ryan and I had done and see the unmistakable stains of truth.

That day of the raid, my family and I waited for the secrets of the basement to be revealed. My mother and I watched everything from the hill in my grandparents' yard. We saw ATF agents removing the machines from the basement on dollies.

"Those must be his machines," my mother said. "I remember when he called me once and told me that he could cure your father."

"Would you have ever tried it?" I asked.

"Are you kidding? I wouldn't believe a word that man said."

In a way, I thought then that believing in Hartley Oden's machines might be no less futile than believing in what Dr. Fawcett or Rev. Goodman had said. The new life the doctors had promised my dad beyond his bone marrow transplant didn't happen. The understanding that Rev. Goodman had assured me did not come. Instead, I silently questioned why my father ever got cancer, why he left my mother and me alone, and why the medicine failed. But I remained a willing believer in Hartley Oden's farm machines: though they disappeared that day of the raid, never to be seen again, at least they had never failed to deliver on their promises.

Twenty-four

Lucky died the summer after my freshman year of college. One evening, while I worked on what I believed would become my first novel, my mother stood in the doorway of my bedroom and stared at me for a moment.

"Guess what," she said.

I looked from the computer screen and noticed something odd about her face. I couldn't tell if she held back tears or laughter.

"Lucky died," she said.

"Yeah. Right."

She stared, unblinking. "No, he's really dead."

I looked back at the computer screen, unsure how to react. Crying seemed the proper thing, but the news struck me with great relief, as if our lives had been cured of a burning scourge. I hadn't seen my grandfather in years—I couldn't even remember the last time, or the last thing he had said to me. His words that day at the hospital after my dad had been diagnosed with cancer, however, did come back to me: "Hell of a thing, outliving your own son." He had been right.

"He died this afternoon," my mother said. "Maybe his heart just gave out."

"What heart?" I asked.

My mother shook her head and glanced around my bedroom. "Don't talk that way. You know your father wouldn't want that."

It was true. My dad never spoke a bad word about his father.

"I suppose we have to go to the funeral?"

"You know we have to," she said. "Your father would want you to go."

It seemed a joke. People went to funerals to pay respect, to honor the dead. I understood that I would have to attend because my father couldn't—I had to represent him in some way. But I would have to pretend to be upset, pretend that Lucky actually meant something to me, something good and positive.

My mother continued standing in the doorway, as if waiting for something. She bit her lower lip. "There's something I never told you about Lucky," she said.

"He really wasn't my grandfather?" I asked hopefully.

She smiled and said, "Come on." She paused and then told me about a great-uncle who had worked for the telephone company in Lewistown. In the early eighties, my uncle, Nena's brother, had been sent to repair something inside the Coleman Hotel. When he walked into the basement, he saw several full gasoline cans in the corner and a pile of oil soaked rags next to them. He deduced that my grandfather intended to burn the place down. My uncle lived in McVeytown and knew about Lucky Varner. He confronted Lucky and threatened to call the police.

"That's true?" I asked.

"Yes," she said.

My stomach felt like a cold knot had formed inside it. I remembered those Friday night visits to the Coleman Hotel with my father, the scores of unshaven derelicts who sweated alcohol. They lived inside that hotel; Lucky could have killed them. I imagined Lucky standing across the street from the Coleman and watching windows blow out from the heat, a hand jingling the change in his pocket, a toothpick in his mouth, and that smirk on his face. Lucky suddenly seemed even worse than I ever realized.

"Did Lucky get in trouble?" I asked. "Was he arrested?"

"I'm not sure what happened after that," she said. "That's all I ever found out."

I wondered how much I didn't know about Lucky's life, or my father's for that matter, and I hated that I would probably never know the entire story. All of what I knew came from my mother, or from Pap and Nena; what they knew had come from mainly secondhand sources. My mother told me that my dad rarely spoke about his childhood, the years before they met—he seemed ashamed and embarrassed. And so the questions lingered.

"How did Lucky and Helen ever buy that hotel in the first place?" I asked.

"I don't know how they bought anything. The insurance company didn't give them any money after that second house burned because the investigators proved it was arson."

I looked back at my computer screen and read a few lines from my novel. If I wrote a novel about Lucky, none of my friends in the creative writing department at college would ever believe it—too contrived, they would say. But all of it had happened—in some inexplicable and horrific way, all of it had happened.

"You know, he was accepted back into this community," my mother said. "He went to church, he had friends. People forgave him."

"But they knew," I said. "They knew what he had done. All they had to do was drive here and look at those two houses, that workshop."

How could McVeytown forgive or forget Lucky's crimes? Many in town still ignored my mother when they saw her. They still resented her for not having a fireman's funeral for my father, and that had been ten years earlier. It seemed absurd. It felt unfair. But at least Lucky would never strike another match. I looked up at my mother and smiled, almost laughing.

She narrowed her eyes. "What?"

"I hope it's hot enough for him," I said. I stomped my foot a few times and looked at the floor. "You like the flames down there?"

My mother pursed her lips and turned, walking down the hallway toward the kitchen.

"Think they'll cremate him? A little fire for old times' sake," I said.

. . .

Lucky wore a suit in his casket. Even in death, he still had that same smirk, as if somehow he had gotten the last laugh. Both of my uncles eulogized their father. They spoke about his nickname—his birth certificate read Simon Varner, though everyone knew him as Lucky. It seemed fitting, both of them said, because Lucky had indeed been lucky throughout his life—he prospered as a carpenter, had three sons and a loving wife.

I elbowed my mother and rolled my eyes.

Helen sobbed throughout the service. Her shoulders were now hunched and her sons had to help her walk. At the end of the service, they led her to the casket. She wept and cried out, "Oh Lucky." She crumbled to the ground and wailed.

My mother and I walked away from the church as if escaping from jail. I couldn't leave the family behind fast enough.

"What a sad old woman," I said. "She deserves this. She deserves to sit alone, without Lucky, and think about what she did."

"Do you have to talk like that?" my mother said. "I know they're terrible, but she loved him."

"But she's no better than him. What she did to Dad? She pushed him into the fire company."

"Yes she did," my mother said. "I know."

Helen almost seemed like my father's Lady Macbeth, full of direst cruelty and ready to push her son into the fire company for the sake of her and Lucky. Their damned spots sat in our yard still, the remnants of the house and the garage. What was done could not be undone.

I turned to my mother. "What if Dad hadn't gone to all those fires? What if he hadn't breathed all that smoke? Maybe he'd still be here. All of it's as much her fault as it is Lucky's. She led him toward the firehouse. She loved what he did because it made her look good and it made Lucky look good." I stopped, panting for breath. My heart raced. I swallowed and laughed, hoping to calm my rant.

"You're supposed to forgive people," my mother said.

"I can't forgive them," I said. "I won't."

Not long after Lucky died, Helen sold their home outside McVeytown and moved into a nursing home. My uncles, Curt and Russ, cleared the furniture out of the house and boxed dishes and books. One Saturday morning, they called me and said that they had a box of things that had belonged to my father. They had almost thrown the box away, but then they wondered if I might want it. So I drove to that house and talked to my uncles. They were both older now, with graying hair and paunchy stomachs, and neither looked much like my father. They asked me the usual questions about my college major and my interests. When I told them that I played guitar, they both smiled.

"Your dad would have loved that," Russ said. "The three of us used to play together every weekend. Man, those were fun times."

"Your dad could tear through 'Pipeline' on his electric guitar," Curt said.

We looked at each other for a few moments, searching for something else to talk about. Aside from blood, we shared very little. I wondered how often they still thought of my father, or about Lucky's fires. Finally, Russ handed me a heavy cardboard box. I thanked them both for calling me.

That night, the first things I found inside the box were some of my old school pictures from elementary and middle school—even after my dad died, I still gave one to Helen and Lucky each year. The photos were folded and ripped, as if they had been carelessly thrown into a kitchen drawer.

Next, I found a letter dated November 1, 1978, from one of my father's friends, who had lived in Texas, a man named Carl Garver. He had addressed it to Lewistown, where my dad lived with his parents. I read the letter aloud to my mother—she vaguely remembered my father talking about a Carl who had moved to Texas to become a state trooper. He wrote to my father about longing for the "Varner-Garver talks" about what was "really happening" in Mifflin County. It reminded me of the talks my cousin Trevor and I had about our hometown.

"You know what, Dent?" Carl wrote. "I never really grew up with the idea of leaving home as soon as I did but things kind of happen and all of a sudden one finds himself looking in a mirror and reflecting back on how quickly everything happens. I never appreciated McVeytown and its people as much as I did when I left."

He signed the letter "Goober."

The friendship between Goober and my father expressed in the letter left me with an empty feeling. I still missed him. Adolescence was long behind me, the time when parents always seemed at odds with their children. If he were still alive, it felt like we would have been good friends.

I continued sifting through the box, digging deep into my father's late teenage years. I read the program for my father's Eagle Scout ceremony, held on January 29, 1973—he would have been seventeen then. In the brief biography printed inside, I learned that my dad had played soccer, was a member of McVeytown United Methodist Church, was a junior fireman, and was already in training to become an ambulance attendant. Among the merit badges he had earned in Boy Scouts were lifesaving, safety, first aid, and firemanship.

The next year, my father graduated from Rothrock High School—the program, dated June 3, 1974, included the names of his sixty-two classmates. I also read his report cards—most of his classes senior year focused on industrial arts such as mechanical drawing and drafting. He carried a B– average throughout high school.

Not surprisingly, many of the things in the box shed light on my father's burgeoning obsession with fire.

There were the notes he kept about firefighting, incredibly a four-page outline of how to prevent and fight fires. The papers weren't dated, but I assumed it had been work for his Boy Scouts' firemanship badge.

"Heat, fuel, and air are the only objects needed for fire," he wrote. "Without air, a fire would suffocate. Without fuel, a fire would have nothing to burn." He listed the five principal causes of fire: heating equipment, careless smoking, faulty wiring, mishandling flammable liquids, and children playing with matches. "Keep matches out of reach of children," he warned.

Below this, he drew a map of his house—the second one that Lucky had burned—and labeled the bedrooms for his parents and brothers. He pledged that if "a small fire should start" in the house, he would attempt to control the flames until the fire department arrived.

The pages of notes ended abruptly with another cause of fire: "Arson — police investigation." After that, his scoutmaster wrote a note that said my dad knew "how to clear an area and start a fire and also how to put a fire out and leave the area in better condition than when he first went there." I reread those words, amazed at their premonition — my dad placed the double-wide on the foundation of one of the houses Lucky had burned.

As I looked closer at that piece of paper, I noticed the left edge looked brown, almost singed. I found a small pamphlet published by the Boy Scouts of America titled "Firemanship." The paper cover looked brown as well, as if it had been placed near heat. Then I realized that they had survived that second fire — my grandfather's flames had licked my father's notes, the pamphlet. My father's Bible had even been burned — I found it in a plastic bag, coverless and with the first several pages burned off. This is something to pass on to a child, I thought.

I read birthday cards friends had sent him, letters and bulletins from the Boy Scouts, newspaper clippings of his high school classmates, and Valentine's Day cards my mother had given him. At the bottom of the box, I found an anonymously written poem that had been read at his Eagle Scout ceremony. I never discovered who chose this poem for the ceremony or why, but I believed the words held special relevance to my father. I imagined reading it through his eyes and thinking about all that Lucky had destroyed in their lives.

Tearing Down or Building Up

I watched them tearing a building down,
A gang of men in a busy town.
With a ho-heave-ho and a lusty yell
They swung a beam and the side wall fell.

I asked the foreman, "Are these men skilled,
And the men you'd hire if you had to build?"
He gave a laugh and said: "No indeed!
Just common labor is all I need.

I can easily wreck in a day or two
What builders have taken a year to do."
And I thought to myself as I went away,
Which of these roles have I tried to play?

Am I a builder who works with care,
Measuring life by the rule and square,
Am I shaping my deeds to a well-made plan,
Or am I a wrecker, who walks the town
Content with the labor of tearing down?

Epilogue

At the end of the year, I decide to resurrect a failed novel I had begun writing in my sophomore year of college, after Lucky had died. It was about a fire chief named Derek Knefler and his arsonist father. On the weekends and the early mornings after I return home from the *Sentinel,* I sometimes rewrite scenes, but something always seems wrong. I write one of my old professors and ask for advice. He writes back and encourages me to abandon the fictionalized story and simply tell the truth. When I finish reading the letter, I place it on the kitchen table, where my mother discovers it.

On a Sunday morning in early January, I walk into the living room to read the Sunday newspapers. Nena and my mother are already sitting on the couch.

"Are you two going to church?" I ask.

"Sit down for a moment," Nena says. "Your mother and I have something we'd like to talk to you about."

I sink into my father's old recliner and wait. They look concerned, and my stomach tenses, preparing for the worst.

"You know that your father was a good man," Nena says. "He was confused, with the fire company and all, but in his heart, he loved you."

"I guess so," I say. He had been good to the fire company and the town, but it seemed that all he ever did for my mother and me was leave. Sometimes, when I heard my friends talk about their fathers, it was hard for me to imagine that my father loved me—I was still angry that the firehouse had robbed so much of his time from me. Yet I knew that he was a deeply conflicted man, pulled in many directions.

"Well, there's something you don't know about your father," my mother says.

For a moment, I think that perhaps all of it—Lucky and his fires—has been a lie. My father had never admitted it, nor had Lucky or Helen. I'd only heard the story from my mother's side of the family. Maybe it has been an elaborate plot, one to turn me against Lucky for some reason. But that doesn't make sense—it wouldn't explain the rubble still left in our yard.

"We never wanted to tell you this," Nena says. "But your mother found that letter your professor wrote to you and—"

My mother interrupts. "Are you writing a book about this family?"

Aside from newspaper articles, I had never shown them a

single word of anything I'd written. We never talked about my father or Lucky; it had become the unspoken and I didn't want to resurrect something my mother clearly didn't want to discuss.

I nod. "I'm writing about it."

"You can't write about it," Nena says. "Can you imagine how your father would react to something like that?"

"Well, no," I say. "I don't know. Sometimes it feels like I didn't know him at all."

Nena looks at the floor and begins to cry. My mother crosses her arms and leans forward, as if nursing a stomach cramp.

"What are you two talking about? I don't get it. What don't I know?" I say.

"Those fires that Lucky set," my mother says, pausing for a moment. "Your father helped Lucky start some of them."

As she tells me the story, I imagine this scene.

One day in the 1960s, probably not long after Lucky burned his car and that shed, Buster, Helen's brother, stopped by to borrow a circular saw from his brother-in-law. He first knocked on the door of the family's house—no answer. Buster looked around for a few moments and then thought he heard laughter coming from inside Lucky's workshop.

As Buster walked closer, he realized that it was young Denton's laugh—an easily recognizable high-pitched giggle. Lucky's probably playing with the kid, Buster thought. He smiled and stepped into the doorway, ready to surprise my father. But instead, he only stood and watched.

Lucky sat on the cement floor of the workshop, holding

Denton, maybe seven years old at the time, in his lap. At first, it looked the two were pushing Matchbox cars on the floor. Lucky patted the mop of brown hair on his son's head.

"That's a good boy," he said. "It's fun, isn't it? Do you like it?"

"Yeah," Denton said, amazement in his voice.

Buster noticed the red and yellow gasoline can that sat next to Lucky. Strange place to put that, he thought. But then he saw what looked like a pool of water on the ground.

Lucky leaned his head toward Denton's, tender and soft, and spoke to him in an almost singsong voice.

"Remember when Daddy's car caught on fire?"

The child nodded.

"There was gasoline in that car," Lucky said. "And it burned so hot. I could feel the heat of the flames. So always be careful with fire. You can get hurt very, very badly."

Denton looked at Lucky's face and nodded again.

Lucky pulled a pack of matches from the front of his shirt pocket. He struck the match and it hissed to life.

"Watch what happens when fire touches the gasoline," Lucky said.

Lucky dropped the match onto the small pool—*poof.* The flames danced for a few minutes and then burned out.

"Whoa," Denton said. "That's cool."

Lucky smiled. He bounced the boy on his knee a few times until he laughed. "You like that? You think you'd like to try it?"

"Yeah," Denton said.

"Lucky Varner," Buster shouted, making his presence known.

My grandfather turned, thrust the child onto the floor, and then scrambled to his feet. "We were just playing," Lucky said.

Buster, strong from growing up on a farm, grabbed the back of Lucky's neck.

"Dad," Denton cried.

Buster pushed Lucky through the open door and then shoved him onto the ground.

Lucky lay still for a few moments.

"You burned your own car?" Buster asked. "Did you burn your car?"

Lucky rolled over and squinted—his glasses had fallen off. He held up a hand, shielding his eyes from the sun, maybe readying himself in case Buster tried to throw a punch.

"Yes," Lucky said.

"Do not ever talk to that boy like that again," Buster said. "If I ever see you talking to him about fire again, I'll kill you. I don't want to ever see you at my house either. You step foot on my property, you're dead."

"Not long after I had you, Buster stopped at our old trailer and told me this story," my mother says. "He thought I should know the truth about Lucky. And he told me to never leave you alone with your grandfather."

"Lucky never went to their house, did he?"

"No," my mother says. "Buster hated him. He said that he would have shot him."

"But how do you know Dad started any fires?"

"Buster said that he did. And that's all he said, just that your father did help Lucky start some of those fires."

We sit in silence a moment. I don't believe what they have

told me. My father had been the fire chief—he didn't start fires, he put them out. It just didn't make sense. Plus, Buster had been an alcoholic. He'd died of cirrhosis not long after my father had been buried. Surely he had concocted the story. But it also makes sense. My father's obsession with the fire company was just a metaphor for how hard he strove to make up for what he had done.

"Did Dad ever tell you that he did it?" I ask.

"No," my mother says. "He never once spoke of it. And I think that even if he hadn't died so young, he still would have taken it to the grave. He wouldn't have told me."

"How many fires did he help start?"

"I don't know. Buster didn't say. He just said that Lucky made your father help."

"Did he help burn their houses down?"

"I don't know," my mother says. "And there's no one left to ask either. I don't even know if Helen knows about this. But she'd never tell you if she did."

So this was why my father had become a fireman, not only to save the family's name but to save himself, to douse his conscience for what he had done. I never understood why he loved that firehouse so much, why he left so often—now I knew.

"Why didn't you ever tell me any of this?" I ask.

"We didn't want you to be mad at him," my mother says. "We were afraid that you would hate him."

"Hate him? I hated that he left all the time, because of that firehouse. But it wasn't his fault. None of it was his fault. Lucky made him like that."

My grandmother shakes her head. "I really felt sorry for your father. He was such a good man. He would give you the shirt off his back. But what that family did to him was terrible. They brainwashed him."

"It was child abuse," I say. Lucky might not have hit my father—though that certainly wouldn't have surprised me—but coaxing his child to set fires went beyond being pathological or cruel. That seemed like pure evil. No wonder my dad's brothers had left so soon after high school; they probably couldn't get away fast enough. Perhaps Lucky had simply wanted my father for a patsy—if the investigators did suspect arson, Lucky could have lied and said his son had done it by accident, or maybe even on purpose. But if that had been his intention, he'd never followed through.

"Don't you see why you can't write about this?" my mother says. "Nobody around here knows about this. A lot of people really liked your father. They'd have never thought he would have done something like this."

"But Mom, he was a kid then," I say. "It wasn't his fault."

I shake my head, stunned by all of this. All the resentment I had held for my father over the years melted to sorrow and pity. I thought of those faith healers on television—they touched the ill on the forehead, and at that instant the sick were supposedly cured. After my mother told me the truth about Lucky and my father, it was as if I could see them both for the first time.

I stand up, walk outside, and look toward the pile of rubble left over from one of the houses Lucky had burned.

. . .

My stories at the *Sentinel* continue to focus on fires and death. More people overdose or are killed in car accidents. One night, a transformer blows up in Lewistown and burns down a garage and part of a house. Lorrie weaves past downed power lines and firemen, snapping photos, while I talk to Lewistown's fire chief, a man I'd heard my father talk about many times.

"Denton Varner?" the chief asks. "Oh, yeah, I remember him. Good fireman and a great man."

I still write the stories, but my obsession seems to fade. After my mother tells me about my father, I no longer feel the need to immerse myself in understanding and sharing the world I cover as a reporter. The fires feel more distant now, as if I have less at stake. Work at the *Sentinel* becomes just a job. But the desire to leave home seems more pressing than ever. In February, Pennsylvania slips into a cold spell with the temperature staying below freezing for thirty-five straight days. I yearn for the warmth of someplace new.

In that dead-cold snap, I drive to an accident scene, walk a half mile over ice and snow, and finally see an upside-down Jeep in a creek bed. The driver lost control on a patch of ice and flipped off the bridge but walked away unscathed. I take a few photos and talk to the police about the specifics so I can write my article.

As I walk away, I see one of my father's old friends, Brad Boyer, the only one who still sent us Christmas cards each year. I remember Brad helping my father work on that old Case lawn mower. One summer afternoon, when a thunderstorm churned across the sky, the three of us waited out the rain and lightning inside the small toolshed my father had built. I remember Brad's frosted white hair and kind blue eyes.

"Brad?"

He turns and smiles. "Jay? I saw your name in the paper. Wondered if I might run into you. How's your mother doing?"

"She's good," I say. "Clips all my articles."

Brad smiles, as if remembering something. He looks me in the eye and says, "You know, your father would have really gotten a kick out of knowing you were covering things like this."

"You think?"

"You kidding me? He talked about you all the time. In fact, I gave him twenty bucks to put into a savings account for you. Do you remember that? Your dad wanted you to have some money set aside for college. Not a day goes by that I don't think about him."

"I know what you mean," I say. "Every time I go to a fire or car accident, I think of him."

"Me too," Brad says. "I miss him. A lot of guys, they still talk about Denton. Can you believe that? Shows you how much he meant to people."

People still fight for Mifflin County—a group of businessmen work to revitalize downtown Lewistown, the school board talks of building a new high school, and the police continue busting drug dealers. As spring warms the air, a glaze of nostalgia seems to set in. Even with its myriad problems, Mifflin County still feels like the only place I could ever live. But finally, I decide that I have to move on, away from my father's shadow and the memories of the town.

I quit the *Sentinel* on the second day of July. My co-workers throw me a party complete with cake and balloons. We exchange e-mail addresses and phone numbers and promise to stay in touch. By five, everyone but the evening shift has left. Throughout that week, I had trained my replacement, a recent college graduate named Nate. He sits at the desk next to mine and types obituaries while I read over police reports.

Nate stops typing and looks at me. He adjusts his glasses and says, "These suck. How many do we usually get?"

"Depends," I say. "Some nights none, other nights a lot. After holidays are the worst. I think people hold off on dying. And if it's a warm Christmas, get ready for the spring."

"Why's that?"

"Green Christmas, fat cemetery," I say. "It's an old saying around here."

"Jesus, that's morbid." He waves a hand at his computer and says, "These are such a waste of news space."

"Look at it this way," I say. "At least everyone will read your work. People always want to know who died."

I wonder how many obituaries I have typed. Around a thousand, I guess. So that calculates into what—maybe ten thousand grief-stricken friends or family members? People never just died: they "passed away," "went to be with their Lord and Savior," "departed their earthly body," or "entered into eternal rest." Their hobbies included quilting, bridge, NASCAR, hunting, CB radios, and model airplanes. For every Allen Groff, James

Van Ness, or Jimmy Cooper, there are dozens of others, anonymous people who died unremarkable deaths.

Alarm codes blast from the scanner and break the silence of the newsroom. I grab a pen and notepad and wait for the dispatcher: a house fire, three fire companies responding. I jump from my chair, open a drawer in my desk and pull out a camera, and tell Nate to come along.

Outside, the humid afternoon air smacks my face. My Tempo squeals around a curve as we speed down a street posted fifteen miles per hour. I descend a hill and watch the light at the intersection change to red. I turn right, cut through a gravel parking lot behind a fast-food restaurant, then jerk the wheel left to reach Electric Avenue. Nate holds on to the dashboard.

"Diagonal rule," I say. "Lorrie taught me that. If a light is red you go diagonal and then turn to get back on your route. It's faster than waiting."

As we drive through Lewistown, I hear the wailing siren of a fire engine behind me. I pull to the side of the road and wait for the truck to pass, then slam the gas and follow the flashing red and white strobe lights.

"It's just like football," I tell Nate. "You find a blocker and gun it. They'll take you right to the end zone."

The diesel exhaust from the fire truck reminds me of the smoky smell that clung to my father's clothes when he returned home from a fire. In the distance, white smoke rises into the blue summer sky. My heart rattles inside my chest. This one will make the front page. The bleeping scanner and then running out the door, the adrenaline rush and the bylines —after today, all of it will be gone.

When we arrive at the fire, I park along the street and watch firemen rush past with hoses over their shoulders. I snap photos of some of the firemen as they climb onto the roof and hack holes through the shingles until deep gray smoke pours up and into the sky. The insides of the house snap. Ash and water spray mix in the air, and for a moment the scene looks almost as serene as a snow shower.

I am carried back to that night when Lucky threw those mattresses from his truck and the Saturday mornings when he poured gasoline into the hole. In my memory, those flames crack and pop, baking whatever junk my grandfather desired to torch. Lucky stands in front of the fire, keeping watch, and the thick black smoke clogs the air, ascending. It lifts into the sky, soaring higher and higher, until there are shadows over all of us.

My mother still wears the silver wedding band on her right hand when she shops for groceries. On anniversaries, she asks me things like "Do you know what happened twenty-four years ago today?" The half-empty bottle of honeysuckle-scented perfume my father bought her for their first Valentine's Day sits on the bureau in her bedroom. She still sleeps on one side of the bed. And the reminders of Lucky still scar our lawn: the pile of rubble excavated from the hole, the cement floor from the garage. The ruin and ashes that define our family still seem too hot to touch.

That summer before I leave McVeytown, we stack firewood for the winter. Pap retired from cutting wood not long after his second hip replacement, so a hired man now brings it by the pickup load. His name is Reggie McDonald and my mother heard about him from one of our neighbors. In the afternoons, after he finishes his day working for a logging company, he drives over old forest roads and deep into the woods, cutting down dead trees. For fifty dollars a truckload, he saws the pieces, splits them, and then for two weeks straight, he delivers them to our house in the evening. My mother calls him the woodman and usually carries him a glass of water when he comes.

One night I watch them out my bedroom window. My mother stands next to him and they talk. She smiles and nods. He leans an arm against the tailgate of his truck; he wears no shirt; his arms and back ripple with hard-earned muscles. Suspender straps sag behind his jeans, which sink low on his waist and, depending on his stance, reveal a slight plumber's crack. He's shaved his head—it looks brown like the rest of his skin, tanned from working days under the sun—and he wears a thick, bushy black beard. He chugs the water from the glass, then wipes his mouth with the back of his wrist.

When he climbs into his truck to leave, my mother walks to the pile of wood he has thrown from the bed of his truck and pretends to sum up the pieces. But she watches him drive out of the driveway, up the hill, and then sink from sight.

She walks back inside the house, my father's double-wide, and says, "The woodman was just here." She smiles and I can feel her excitement. "He's a hard worker. You know, all the money he earns cutting wood for people, he saves it up so he can take trips out West to hunt."

"I bet it's nice out there," I say. "You should go out there sometime."

"Yeah," she says, and rolls her eyes. "I bet that'll really happen."

The next night while I mow grass, Reggie pulls into the driveway. I turn off the old Case garden tractor and walk toward his truck to finally meet him. When he talks, I can see the brown tobacco stains on his teeth. His bare back and torso glisten. The elastic lip of sweat-stained briefs creep up from under his sagging blue jeans. Before he leaves, he offers me his large, calloused hand.

"Nice meeting you," he says.

He walks with a limp toward the cab of his truck, and I ask if he dropped a piece of wood on his foot.

"No, that's 'cause of my toe." He says this without embarrassment or humor. "Lobbed it off with a push mower a few years back. Doctors said my balance won't never be right again."

While my mother and I stack the pieces of wood, she tells me about the hunting trips Reggie takes to Montana, New Mexico, and Wyoming, all of it funded by cutting wood on the side. He has brought her pictures of slaughtered elk and antelope, and photographs of sky-scraping mountains.

"He told me he can't come tomorrow night," my mother says. "He's taking his wife and son up to the Huntingdon County Fair. He wants to see the tractor pull."

"Well, I can't blame him," I say. "That's where I'd want to be on a Saturday night."

"Oh, stop it," she says. "He's a good guy."

"Seems like he is. You never told me he was married. I thought you liked him."

"Oh, you know." She smiles.

But I know she doesn't like him in that way. It's been so long since anyone, let alone a man, paid attention to her, she's just smitten with the chance to interact with someone.

"This doesn't make sense, does it?" she asks. "Stacking wood in this stinking heat just so you can burn it in the winter and not freeze?"

"No, I guess not," I say.

"You know where I wish I was?" She stops and brushes the back of her gloved hand across her forehead to soak up some of the sweat. "Alaska."

"Well, I hate to ruin it for you, but it's cold up there too."

"Yeah, but they say it's supposed to feel like a different kind of cold," she says.

When the sun begins to sink on the western horizon, my mother asks me for the time. I slip off my glove, and press the button for the light on the side of my watch, that same Timex Ironman that Pap had bought for me before my dad died.

Semis hum along the highway and their Jake Brakes patter as they slow to drive through McVeytown, the small kernel of a village where the memory of my father endures. A freight train clanks along the railroad tracks, and the metallic beats echo against the hills. It no longer feels that the world continues to pass by my mother and me, but at this moment I'm not sure that it would even matter. After all that we have been through, my mother and I still have each other. We work silently under a crimson twilight that fires over the ridges, burns across the roof of our double-wide, and then spreads a warm glow that washes across cornfields for miles and miles.

Author's Note

During his eulogy for Helen, my father's brother Curt stood behind the lectern at the front of the funeral home. Before he began to tell stories from her life, he asked a rhetorical question: "I thought yesterday, if I were to write a book on my mother's life, what would I include in each chapter?"

He mentioned her time at the hotel, when this woman with little business experience kept the books and acted as much as a manager as a psychologist for the down-on-their-luck tenants. He said that she had survived the most difficult ordeal of her life, my father's death, with steady resolve and a belief in God. If a friend or neighbor was sick or in the hospital, Helen stopped by for a visit—she never forgot about those who suffered. And no matter what part of the country she was in, Helen would always find the one person at a highway rest stop or restaurant also from Pennsylvania.

But the best story he told was about Helen's fear of water. She wanted to make sure that all of her kids knew how to swim because she had never learned. Of course, I remembered how she encouraged my mother to enroll me for lessons at the local pool one summer. Helen wasn't the prettiest sight in a bathing suit, my uncle said, but she was determined to swim. During her first few attempts at the YMCA, she did little more than flail and splash—she didn't even drift from side to side, somehow staying absolutely immobile. But none of this deterred her. She went back again and again, bent on making some kind of progress. After a while, my uncle thought that it might be time to take her aside, tell her that though she had tried her best, she just wasn't getting anywhere. But finally, one day, she did. Amid the waves of spattering water, the churning arms, her pumping legs, she swam. It was only six feet, but it was something.

"I would want that in a book," my uncle said, wiping away tears.

After the funeral, I spoke with both my uncles, especially Uncle Curt. He was divorced now, though he still lived in Ohio. He asked about what I done in the eight years since I had last seen him at Lucky's funeral. After a half hour or so, when we had run out of news to share, there was a silence. He asked for my contact info, telling me that Helen and Lucky had left an insurance policy behind for me since my father had died, and said that he would send the information. A month later, he called to let me know the paperwork was in the mail and asked me what the weather was like in Virginia.

As I write this final note, nearly two years have passed since I finished the first manuscript, and most in my family still do not know about this book. I've given great thought as to how they will react, along with those in my hometown. Many people there still remember my father—and his parents—fondly. In the case of his mother and father, I do not intend to spoil or ruin what others might recall, only to share my experience and hope that it sheds a greater light on the events many already know. Though questions in this story will never be answered, I know for certain that everything my father did was with the best of intentions. It took years for me to reconcile with the times the fire company pulled him away from our family. This book, I hope, shows his motivations, pulls back the curtain on the very public life he led in our town, and helps explain why he sacrificed so much for so many.

My mother might not have rushed off into the night or sawed open crushed automobiles. She never drove through town in a parade. But she taught me to unapologetically stand by the right decision, even when an entire town disagrees with you. Though she would never speak up in a crowd, my mother has the strongest voice of anyone I know. She raised a son, largely on her own, but also with the help of two loving, remarkable grandparents.

My mother only asked that I include one thing in this book. She wants it made clear to everyone in our hometown that she urged me to write none of this. I understand her concern—the town is small and people talk. Unlike me, my mother still lives near there and she worries that many will wonder why she ever told me these stories about our family. And, most important, I

Acknowledgments

Thank you to Daniel Lazar. I can't imagine a better agent. You're a tireless fighter, an excellent reader, and a wonderful human being. Plus, you answer every question with humor and grace.

Also, thanks to everyone else at Writers House who contributed their guidance and expertise.

Chuck Adams, you deserve more than a simple thank you. You believed in me and this book. And through it all, you have given me the very best. I am forever indebted.

Also, thanks go out to Ina Stern, Craig Popelars, Michael Taeckens, Courtney Wilson, and everyone else at Algonquin who helped.

David Gessner offered relentless enthusiasm, interest, and encouragement. He gave me just the right push when I needed it the most.

Clyde Edgerton and Phil Furia offered wonderful insights and lessons.

Wendy Brenner always e-mailed me back within minutes, no matter what.

Also, thanks to Rebecca Lee, Philip Gerard, Tim Bass, Nina de Gramont, Megan Hubbard, and everyone else at the University of North Carolina, Wilmington.

John Jeremiah Sullivan, Virginia Holman, and Bill Roorbach all read various and partial drafts of this book. Your thoughts and encouragement were invaluable.

Thanks to the staff of *Ecotone: Reimagining Place*.

Gary Fincke and Tom Bailey at Susquehanna University. You were truly the first people to encourage me. I would not have typed any of these words if not for you. Not a day passes when I don't think of something I learned in class or in the basement of Hassinger Hall.

Also, thanks to Karen Holmberg, Kate Hastings, Amy Winans, Mary Bannon, Susan Bowers, Mark Fertig, and Crystal VanHorn at Susquehanna.

Adam Cole, Nick Ripatrazone, Mark Martelli, Katelen Marr, Devon Persing, Zach Macholz, Jenny Ruth Binger, Hannah Gilbert, Shanna Powlus Wheeler, Josh Lapekas, and all of my peers at Susquehanna offered great advice and friendship.

For the current and former Wilmington crop: Chris McSween, Jake Hinkson, Bill Carty, Bryan and Heather Sandala, Ben and Emily Gorman-Fancy, Adam Petry, Doug Bourne, Emily Smith, Lauren Breeden Hodges, Miriam Parker, Hannah Dela Cruz Abrams, Jason and Lauren Frye, Rory Laverty, David and Jo Howell, Sumanth Prabhaker, Joel Moore,

Patricia Moyer, Julie Overman, Douglas Cutting, Emily Self Brown, Heather Hamilton, Kirsten Holmstedt, Louisa Jonas, MaryEllen Martino, Tom Kunz, Matt Tullis, Stephanie J. Andersen, Stevie Lynne Kohler, Visha Burart, Xhenet Aliu, Daisy Barringer, Erin Bond, Gwendolyn Knapp, Chris Malpass, Lindsey Ronfeldt, Shawna Kenney, Rich Dolinger, Brad Land, Eric Vithalani, and everyone else I should have listed. Without all of them, I would have never survived the Dub.

Gabe Spece has attended many (and hopefully more) Pearl Jam concerts with me, read all the drafts of this book and everything else, and this is just the beginning.

Patrick Culliton answers the phone every time I call. He's the only Buckeye I've ever befriended, and coming from a Penn State fan, that's saying something.

Matt and Luke Primak—you guys taught me how to play music, and much more.

Andrew Kissinger will probably never room with a moody writer again.

Eric Mowery heard all of this before over countless cups of coffee at Red's.

Matt Rutherford still debates politics with me.

And of course Frank Grimes.

Elaine Siddons took a chance on a shy kid out of college and turned him into a better writer, as she did with so many other reporters.

Susie Kozar can still call me "Jaybird," no matter what.

Carey Goodman, Jamie Estes, Lorri Freitas, and Southern Teachers Agency.

I owe Adam Peichert about $200 in gas money.

Mifflin County, Pennsylvania—despite it all, I still love you.

My cousins Travis, Jeremy, and Jason—you are like my brothers.

To my family. There are so many others who have impacted my life with their care, support, and kindness.

Pap and Nena—no words can ever express proper thanks for all that you've done and the love you've given me.

To my mother. Somehow, we made it through all of this. I believe it was only because we had each other. You never wanted me to write this story and perhaps you'll never even make it so far as to read this. I only hope that I got this right. Despite all his flaws, my dad was still a great man who always tried to do what was right. If I ever become half the man he was, it will be because of your love.

And to my wife, Danielle DeRise, the reader I value most. Your support, comments, encouragement, and love drove me to become a better writer and person. Each day might be possible without you, but none of them would be worth as much.